NO MONEY? NO PROBLEM!

The Royaloak Story

VIJAI SUBRAMANIAM

STARDOM BOOKS

www.StardomBooks.com

STARDOM BOOKS
112 Bordeaux Ct.
Coppell, TX 75019, USA

Copyright © 2024 by Vijai Subramaniam

All rights reserved. No part of this book may be reproduced or used in any manner without written permission of the copyright owner except for the use of quotations in a book review.

FIRST EDITION MARCH 2024

STARDOM BOOKS, LLC.
112 Bordeaux Ct. Coppell, TX 75019, USA

www.stardombooks.com

Stardom Books, United States
Stardom Alliance, India

The author and publishers have made all reasonable efforts to contact copyright holders for permission and apologize for any omissions or errors in the form of credits given. Corrections may be made to future editions.

No Money? No Problem!
Vijai Subramaniam

p. 227
cm. 13.5 X 21.5

Category:
BUS025000 Business & Economics: Entrepreneurship
BUS071000 Business & Economics: Leadership

ISBN: 978-1-957456-42-3

FOREWORD

Dear Reader,

Step into the enthralling world of Vijai Subramaniam, an extraordinary entrepreneur & Chairman of Royaloak Furniture, whose journey is as an example to the extraordinary heights achievable through undulating determination, relentless hard work and a profound passion for one's craft. Being his brother is of the greatest blessings of my life.

In the pages that follow, you'll become immersed in the heartfelt story of Vijai's journey—a story that goes beyond business, touching the very soul of the human spirit. Discover why countless others, myself included, hold deep admiration and respect for him. The book unfolds the power of following one's heart and trusting instincts—a universal lesson that resonates with dreamers of all kinds.

Embark on a nostalgic journey through the formative years that shaped Vijai's character and fueled his ambition, laying the foundation for the remarkable success story behind the household name, Royaloak. This book paints a vivid picture of the heartbreaks and disappointments that forged Vijai's grit and resilience, defining his entrepreneurial spirit. It shares the inspiring tale of overcoming setbacks and transforming challenges into opportunities, revealing how he navigated the ever-evolving world of design and innovation.

Offering glimpses into the personal and professional facets of my brother's life, this book highlights his dedication to his work and unveils aspects of his personality that only handful of people are privy to.

As you delve into these pages, you will not only glean valuable lessons from Vijai's life but also find the inspiration to chase your dreams. Functioning as a guide for aspiring entrepreneurs, the book stresses on a crucial lesson: capital isn't the primary resource needed to kick- start your business.

It serves as a handbook for applying positive thinking in real life, illustrating how a positive mind set propels individuals to the pinnacle of success. Turn the pages and start this remarkable journey with Vijai—this book is a roadmap to achieving remarkable success through the driving force of passion and the guidance of intuition.

Happy reading!
Mathan Subramaniam

CONTENTS

	Acknowledgments	i
	Introduction	1
1	Driven by Passion, Guided by Intuition	5
2	Memories That Could Never Fade	29
3	Brewing Success Through Hard Work And Consistency	53
4	A Singapore Nightmare: Surviving Despite All The Setbacks	71
5	The Exhibition Triumph: A Path To Transformation	89
6	The Turning Point	111
7	Accomplishing Professional Goals At An Early Age: A Trip To China	137
8	Billion-Dollar Business With Zero Investment	159
9	Seeing Tomorrow, Today	179
10	Unwrapping Inspiration: A Chapter for Young Minds	199
	Conclusion	211
	About the Author	215

ACKNOWLEDGMENTS

In the quiet moments of reflection that brought this book to my life, I find myself overwhelmed with gratitude for the incredible individuals who have woven the threads of my journey. Each word on these pages is a proclamation to the strength that emerges within you when love, support and resilience unite.

To my brother Mathan & parents, you are the anchors of my life. Your unchanging love and support have been the core on which I built the foundation of my life. I am forever in debt to the sacrifices you made and the lessons you have taught, shaping me into the person I am today.

To my wife and children, you are the rhythm that fills my every day with joy. Your presence fills my life with purpose and your belief in me drives me to overcome any obstacle I face. I am eternally grateful for the love and motivation you bring into my world, inspiring me to strive for greatness.

To my friends, you are the cherished chapters in the story of my life. Your camaraderie and laughter have been the sweet melodies that have eased me during my challenging times. Thank you for reminding me that life is not just about reaching destinations but savoring the journey and smelling the roses every once in a while.

A big thank you to Anurita Manj, David J K, Riju Paulose and Jai Prakash Giri for being the backbone of this book's creation.

Lastly, thanks a lot to our Royaloak family. Your presence has enriched my journey.

It is like flipping through the pages of your favorite album, each one filled with good times and memories together. We are making a story that goes beyond what is written in this book.

I am sure that, with all of you beside me, we can achieve amazing things. In the big picture of life, your contributions have made something really wonderful, and I feel grateful for the fulfillment you have brought to my life.

This book belongs to all of us, not just me. It shows how powerful it is when we go through things together, build lasting connections and tap into the strong spirit within each of us.

With heartfelt gratitude,

Vijai Subramaniam.

INTRODUCTION

Picture this: you live under the extreme oppression of poverty, not a single rupee in your pocket, yet dream of starting your own business. What would you do if you desperately wanted to fulfill that dream without knowing where to begin?

We all come from places where people believe money is the only important thing in the world. Growing up, I had seen some city people invest tons of money into businesses and become rich pretty quickly. Others respected these entrepreneurs immensely — getting up from their chairs and bowing whenever they saw the rich folks passing by the road. So, on one hand, there were these hotshots who commanded respect wherever they went. On the other hand, there were people like me who struggled hard to afford a day's meal.

Although we hadn't harmed anyone around and lived a very simple life, we received not even the bare minimum amount of respect. Most of my relatives lived moderately luxurious lives, so they felt embarrassed to invite us to their parties and events. My mother ran a tiny, tin-roofed shop in our village, which was our only income source.

Each time it rained, our house got drenched in the water that seeped through the walls. My brother and I had to squeeze our dripping vests dry before going to school every day because we hardly had three shirts. We often exchanged them among us until they were full of holes. It may seem that I felt embarrassed by my circumstances or ashamed of that life, but I never did.

I was unabashed about every hole in my shirt, the streams of water that rushed into our house during monsoon, the chewiness of the roti, and the soil muddying our drinking water.

When most of my friends complained about not having fancy homes, I was not dismayed to tell them that we never even had electricity. We never had a cozy bed or a chair to sit on. However, we found our rustic home quite luxurious and were grateful for everything we had.

Walking through the town, I used to look into every nice shop, wondering how they could sell such fancy things. Where do they get those ultra-luxury products from? My mother used to sell homemade pickles and sweets, so I never knew about terms like "importing" and "exporting" or about entrepreneurship or how it worked back then.

Growing up, the only thought I had was to help my mother and rescue our family from the grip of privation. I worked hard and studied all day and night despite having a lot of limitations, hoping that life would change one day.

And now, after over three decades, I stand before you as a testament to the indomitable human spirit. A successful entrepreneur, a name known far and wide, with an annual turnover that eclipses the dreams of my youth. This book is about my journey from being a broke young boy to becoming a victorious magnate.

Do you think you need to be loaded with wealth to become an entrepreneur? If yes, I'm here to prove you wrong and guide you in the right direction; I will help you achieve what you have been looking forward to fulfilling all these years.

I might be coming from a place where I had to starve all week, but today, I am capable enough to feed thousands of starving people. Royaloak did not grow like a wild tree that sprouted from a seed accidentally thrown into the soil. It took us copious amounts of time and patience to transform it into what it looks like today. It's not always about the money. It's about the strength to fight against all odds to achieve what you never thought you could. It's about proving that you are not afraid of challenges and that nothing under and beyond the sky is impossible.

Several people would try to pull you down, trip you over, and then laugh from a corner. But you must stay confident and trust your skills rather than giving undue importance to somebody else's misbehavior.

Betrayal is a wound that cuts deeper than any physical pain, and I have felt its sting searing through my very soul. My uncle, a figure I once trusted implicitly, thrust the dagger of deceit into my heart. The repercussions were not merely emotional; they reverberated through the very fabric of my entire existence, inflicting a devastating hit on my financial situation.

I trusted him and gave him all my hard-earned money, thinking he would rescue me from my hardships, as promised. But things turned upside down when I realized I would not get a good life or my money back. Each coin lost was a blow to the tireless efforts of my mother and me, for each coin was forged with the sweat and toil of our weary bodies.

Our hard-earned money, a symbol of our hopes and dreams, was callously snatched away, leaving a void that could never be filled. But we still survived, and that is why I insist you never pay much heed to people's opinions or behavior. Life is unpredictable, and you do not know when fortune will come. You have to keep your doors open to let it in.

This book is a chronicle of my extraordinary journey—an ode to the triumph of a once-broken young boy who rose to become a victorious individual.

Together, let us embark on this extraordinary journey—a tale of hope, resilience, and the boundless potential within each of us. Within these pages, you will find inspiration to shatter the shackles that bind you to rise above the limitations that society has imposed.

This story will touch your heart and ignite the embers of possibility within your soul. For in the face of adversity, we discover our true potential and pursue the creation of a legacy that transcends our humble beginnings.

So, join me in this exploration of the extraordinary. Let me take you through the lessons of weaving the threads of hope and determination into a tapestry of triumph. For within our hearts lies the power to transform our lives and prove that, against all odds, we can forge a future full of greatness.

1
DRIVEN BY PASSION, GUIDED BY INTUITION

"The gem cannot be polished without friction, nor man perfected without trials."
- Chinese Proverb

Have you ever felt lost in a never-ending loop, not knowing what to do next? Have you been too scared to rescue yourself from a conflict? Have you felt that there is nothing more you can do to solve an issue or turn an unfavorable situation around? Well, there isn't a single human who might not have gone through a feeling like that. I'll tell you a story- a story of tears, of pain, of resilience, of patience, of never-ending hard work, and of rising from the ashes like a phoenix. They say we only live once, but in reality, we only die once. We live every day. Or should I say that we must live every day irrespective of the uncertainty that looms around the corner to come out of the loop we're stuck in?

Life is complex and utterly unpredictable, to say the least. It is fickle, and no one can ever fathom the unforeseen future. Miracles or misery, anything can sweep us away from the normalcy of life. We can never know when an otherwise mundane day metamorphoses into something utterly surprising. All we can do is sit back and watch as our life plays out in front of our eyes like a movie. The only difference is that it is not a Kamal Hassan or Rajinikanth movie; we are the protagonists of our lives, pondering over an unknown and never-read-before script.

Although the unpredictability of life sometimes becomes intimidating, there lies a peculiar beauty in the unforeseen future. A new surprise awaits every day. No matter how much we prepare for what is to come, life will take turns and twists, putting us in the right place at the right time. To see multiple facets of life is both frightening and exciting. It adds spice and joy to this beautiful journey of life.

Now, when the future is uncertain, we can assume it as a blank canvas, and thus, we are bestowed with the chance to create something new every day. We can choose to take umpteen risks and explore the unknown. As the famous American writer Paul Auster said — *The world is unpredictable. Things happen suddenly, unexpectedly. We want to feel we are in control of our existence. In some ways, we are, and in others, we're not. The forces of chance and coincidence rule us.*

Uncertainty is an integral element attached to life. Nothing knocks on our door with surety; however, we can choose courage and optimism to live a content life. Having said that, not every courageous act or optimistic approach can lead us to a desirable outcome. All our plans can go for a toss in front of the unpredictability of life. And then there comes the masterstroke of destiny.

Do we know what we are destined for? No. We are pushed headfirst into many choices, and what we choose from the mayhem decides our future. What if we choose something that gets us into the worst possible aisle of outcomes? We have the ability and authority to choose our path, and if our choices leave out a big room for mistakes, all we can do is learn from them and grow further with the knowledge gained. A journey filled with surprises can never be chalked out with a fool-proof plan. Success, failure, hurdles, and challenges remain our companions in this ever-changing, unpredictable, and beautiful life.

While talking about the unpredictability of life, there cannot be a better example than the COVID-19 pandemic. The year 2020 came in carrying the promise of a new dawn. Like every year, the world was preparing to welcome the new year with spirit and might, determined to make it all count.

The year took off with high energy and optimism. However, within a few months, a drastic change, utterly unimaginable, knocked at our threshold. COVID-19 cast its shadow over the entire planet. The mere struggle to survive was omnipresent. COVID-19 took over a million innocent lives in the blink of an eye. From the poor to the rich, every human witnessed an intractable change in their lives. Business empires began to collapse like a house of cards. Entrepreneurs were choking under debt and liabilities, while every other day, an organization sank deeper into an unfathomable and irrevocable pit of despair.

As employers failed, employees had to bear the brunt of everything. People were fired from their jobs, and businesses teetered on the edge of bankruptcy. Every human being breathed despair and desperation as the entire population crawled arduously through the agonizing catastrophe. Gradually, as the dawn and the dusk played hide and seek, the world had metamorphosed, rather mutated, into a new avatar. The capricious cloak of life stood exposed in front of all of us.

Going by world history, the year 1918 hosted a similar life-and-death situation. Considering the absence of technology and medical advancement, the situation was far more brutal. Lives were snatched amidst the prevailing ignorance toward an unknown virus.

While in 2020, we knew about the virus, its symptoms, and everything, there lingered a trace of anonymity in the air like a translucent mist, masking the faces of those who walked the streets. In the wake of this pandemic, human life stood under an ominous cloud of death and darkness. Who could imagine we would wake up one fine day, and the first necessity would be wearing a mask? Who could imagine that we would all struggle to recognize our loved ones behind that mask?

While treading in the proverbial way, we do say that all humans are masked, for they reveal different colors in different situations. But then, all of a sudden, life took such a toll on our existence that wearing a mask became an unchangeable routine. For good or for bad, we all had to wear masks. Somehow, owing to the bewildering predicament we were all in, we felt extremely disconnected. Even the ones closest to us began to look like strangers.

Soon enough, everyone was shivering with the fear of contracting the disease; gone were the days of get-togethers. Everyone, be it a Hollywood star or a daily wage laborer, was imprisoned within the four walls of their houses.

Unpleasant emotions kept piling up in the form of negativity and fear as we lived secluded, far away from social life. "What if we die tomorrow? What would happen to our families? What if we lose our well-paying job?" Life dragged through all kinds of what-ifs, and nothing positive seemed to happen.

It was indeed disheartening and confounding for me to wake up to the headlines that mentioned that we were not supposed to step out of our houses for weeks. With the clock ticking, darkness and despair grabbed us by our collars. The world was thrown into chaos by a seemingly invisible enemy, creating visible tears in the tapestry of society.

A microscopic virus, something that we could never see through our eyes, was deciding the daily routines of millions. The whole world came to a standstill. We were prohibited from going to work, school, or visiting friends and family. We were not allowed to go to the movies or out to dinner. We were not even allowed to take a walk in the park.

Humans are social animals; logically, we can never live like this. It was so strange and mind-boggling, something that the present generation had never experienced anything like this before. Scared and confused, we kept weaving thoughts that never made sense but did kindle fear constantly.

While everyone around me was appalled about this lockdown and COVID wreaking havoc on our lives, I tried to stay calm. We have all been in moments when our emotions have gotten the better of us, triggering an outburst of anger, sadness, or fear. But once we learn to stay calm, even in the most trying times, our reactions can become much more effective, and Newton's third law will take a backseat. The first step to staying calm is to become aware of our feelings.

Knowing what we feel and why we feel like that can help us see the situation more objectively and give us the space to make thoughtful decisions. When we recognize our emotions, we should take deep breaths and practice mindfulness or meditation.

Taking a few moments to relax our bodies and clear our minds can help us remain in control of our emotions. Another way to stay calm is to focus on our thoughts. Negative thoughts lead us nowhere but to the deepest den of insecurity. Even in the most difficult times, we must challenge and replace those thoughts with more positive ones. Instead of ruminating on a problem, we can focus on solutions.

How can we solve a problem if we keep nourishing the same line of thought that had pitched the problem? Life is and shall remain a bag full of problems, and instead of lingering on the probabilities of what can go wrong, we must seek solutions. Taking a step back and gathering a new perspective is sometimes helpful.

It is not unusual to be overwhelmed as adversity strikes. Taking a break can help us clear our minds and better understand the situation.

However, it is always easier said than done. The COVID pandemic was yet another challenge for us; somehow, we believed the world would soon overcome it. Royaloak was South India's top furniture company until 2020. So, people around me were earnestly concerned about the organization's future. However, we were never apprehensive about the aftermath of the pandemic as we believe there is always an energy surrounding us that guides us through all the obstacles, no matter how terrible or big.

As the virus marched against time, the chances of the business collapsing seemed quite strong.

However, I was sure I had the skills to weave everything again from scratch with the support of my entire team. I was least bothered about what was in store; however, the feeling was not the same for our team at Royaloak. The pandemic had cast a pall of fear and uncertainty, causing deep trepidation among our teammates. The virus had infiltrated, shaking the foundations of the security they had come to rely on.

A hazy fog of doubt and anxiety had replaced the usual certainty around employment, financial security, and career growth. For those with children, there was the added worry of providing for their families as bills continued to mount and incomes dwindled. For those living alone, the fear of isolation and loneliness was pervasive, with physical distancing rules making it hard to stay connected with the outside world.

Our team was uncertain about the future, unsure how long the pandemic would last and how it would affect their lives and livelihoods. They felt helpless and powerless as the virus spread and the death toll rose. As their leader, I had to be a patient listener to their worries and also a reliable counselor. I tried to calm them down, and my mantra was to ask them to avoid stalking the news occasionally. Truthfully, the news channels further instigated the fear with a constant reality check.

We could only speculate about the future and its repercussions. Every day, we were presented with new challenges and obstacles that impeded our progress and our attempts to return to some semblance of normalcy.

In the face of this overwhelming adversity, our collective morale faded, and we became increasingly discouraged. We worried about our health, finances, jobs, and the future of our families and communities. We wondered how long this situation would last and the long-term consequences of the pandemic. The more we thought about the aftermath, the more discouraged we became. We could realize that the economic impact of the pandemic would be felt for years to come, and many of us were struggling to find a way forward. Moreover, staying positive was a huge struggle. Soon, I asked my squad to start working instead of getting wrapped in their thoughts to distract them from the hellish headlines.

The COVID pandemic and the tragedies that might follow played a horrifying slideshow. As their leader, I had to ensure my people were not demotivated.

An idle mind is the devil's workshop. The more they remained away from work, the more they were invested in the pandemic and its probable aftermath. So, I decided on their resumption of duties. Initially, they couldn't comprehend this request since reports stated that companies were curtailing salaries everywhere.

My team had three questions. The first question that knocked me down was —will we receive our salary? I had no idea how, but I assured them that everything would be just like before the pandemic's onset.

The next question was, "How will you pay us during this situation when we don't know whether or not the company would have proper sales the way it did before COVID?" I was at a loss for words.

However, they had faith in me and agreed to the proposal. The third one was even more serious – "What are we going to work on?" Well, the question made sense.

When the rest of the organizations around us were shutting down, and the world was going through an entire dark phase where we weren't sure whether we would live tomorrow, what would I ask them to work on? I decided to trust my intuition as it said not to worry and that this, too, shall pass. I was confident deep inside and assured them we would find a way out of this tragic situation.

Now, there was another glitch. Our business ran on the traditional mode. Technological intervention was not a regular affair. However, the situation demanded the introduction of new means and interaction methods, which dragged us to the interface of Google Meet and Zoom meetings.

The faces we could see daily while roaming in the corporate aisle were now locked inside the laptop screen. We were all physically separated and connected virtually; interestingly, the roots of our relationship remained strong. Despite being behind the screens, I knew what my people were feeling and going through.

As W.B. Yeats said, *"The world is full of magic things, patiently waiting for our senses to grow sharper."* I firmly believe in a spiritual realm, and at that critical moment, I wanted my people to follow a bit of it to stay fit and mentally stable.

I asked them to meditate and have the remote control of their minds in their own pockets so that they could understand when and where to limit their emotions and stress. I am not a spiritual guru or a yoga expert, but believe me, meditation is a powerful tool; it always helps calm the mind and reduce stress and negative thoughts. It helps to quieten the mind, allowing clarity and a better perspective to rejuvenate. And most importantly, it helps to nurture inner peace.

Feeling overwhelmed with emotions and thoughts can help us step back and observe our situation with a more neutral perspective. It can allow us to be still and observe what is happening in our minds and bodies without judgment. This, in turn, helps us to reduce the intensity of our emotions and to gain a greater understanding of our feelings. Meditating teaches us to observe our thoughts without getting caught up in them. It is more like detangling ourselves from deteriorating thoughts, which helps us be less reactive to difficult situations and approach them more rationally and thoughtfully. Meditation instills the thought of gratitude and appreciation for everything around us. Contentment: that is the outcome of this powerful tool of mediation.

In the same context, I wanted my people to be open to the possibilities rather than remaining tied to negative emotions. Eighty percent of the teammates showed up to the office as per my request since they had faith in me. I have never failed to meet their needs and expectations, and it was like a return favor that they never stopped being loyal to the organization.

I believe that without people, the brand is incomplete, so I am dead against forcing my people. I only requested them to figure out if they could be at work. Had they not shown up, I don't know where we would be now. Still, I would say that I was least bothered about the negative results. Come what may, the only sword that is sharp enough to fight through negativity is the power of positive thinking.

We often underestimate the power of positive thinking. But believe me, it can manifest itself into the reality of a person's life. It is the manifestation of our strongest and most sincere desires and beliefs that can be instrumental in transforming our lives. Positive thinking can take us from darkness to light, from distress to a place of joy and hope. It always opens new doors of possibilities and opportunities. It helps us to focus on the positives and recognize the beauty that is all around us.

For me, the incredible growth of technology was more like a wake-up call to improvise the traditional business method. It was a positive force to drive me on the path of innovation. Technology has become an integral part of our everyday lives, transforming how we interact with each other and the world around us.

This rapid and continuous technological advancement has enabled us to do once-inconceivable things. We can now communicate with anyone in the world in real time, access vast libraries of information from anywhere, and even control our homes from a distance. Technology has also made our lives easier, enabling us to automate mundane tasks and access previously too-expensive or inaccessible services. We can even access virtual realities or explore the ocean's depths from the comfort of our homes. When so many unthinkable things could be achieved using technology, I, too, decided to keep up the trend.

The physical stores of Royaloak were facing a shortage of footfall, and we were left with just Forty Lakh rupees in our account. Also, I had to keep my promise to my workforce by paying them without delay.

Although I promised them, I was not financially sound enough to cover everyone's salary. They knew my bank balance was too low, which worried them about their salaries.

I started pondering on ways to get out of this financial mess. Moreover, I trusted my intuitions more than anything else, for I knew that was the ultimate game changer. After all, like Alen Alda once said, *"At times, you have to leave the city of your comfort and go into the wilderness of your intuition. What you'll discover will be wonderful. What you'll discover is yourself."*

We all have that voice or intuition inside of us that guides us toward decisions and life paths. It is often challenging to trust our intuition, as the world around us constantly sends messages that can conflict with the wisdom within us. Yet, when we take the time to listen to and trust our intuition, we can move to a place of profound understanding and insight.

To discover the unforeseen opportunities that the world holds in its secret chamber, it is necessary to step out of your comfort zone. That is never an easy job to do. It needs immense courage and a brave decision to take the chance to explore the unknown. It is a leap of faith into the unknown, a willingness to take risks and challenge oneself to grow and develop. It is a journey of self-discovery, a chance to break free from the familiar and embrace the unfamiliar.

Stepping out of one's comfort zone can be an intimidating prospect. Fear of the unknown and the fear of failing are the major deterrents to taking the plunge. But it is only by taking the plunge that one can truly grow and develop. You can better understand yourself and the world by pushing yourself out of your comfort zone. It is a process of trial and error. It is a process of learning and growing, of pushing oneself to explore new possibilities and to take risks. It is an opportunity to push boundaries and explore new ideas. It is as if life itself is giving us a chance to discover our hidden talents and capabilities, to try new things, and to gain a greater understanding of everything around us.

Since the digital way of living was the future, it was high time we broke the shell of our conventional methods and embraced the newer things. Royaloak had an official online shopping website. However, we did not concentrate on it before COVID-19 as our physical store sales and revenue were sufficient for all our needs. But the moment the pandemic kicked in, we decided to take care of Royaloak's online store to generate income. I sat down with the team to chalk out a wonderful strategy to bring the plan to reality. What is life if not a journey to bring our wildest dreams to life? We strive to make our plans a reality to feel alive and true to ourselves.

With each step we take along our paths, we discover more of our and the world's potential, as the whole universe is a storehouse of experiences.

My sudden decision to renovate this online store offended the physical franchise owners. As business owners, my younger brother Mathan and I understood their state of mind. They were already facing a huge loss in sales due to the pandemic, and the thought of me restructuring our online store to compete with them must have been disheartening.

However, the world was in complete chaos back then. People were worried about their lives, and furniture was not even in the picture. Ecommerce websites were non-operational due to government restrictions on delivery services, implemented to mitigate the spread of the virus. We were genuinely worried about how the digital business would help us. We had no clue about who would purchase the products. But we decided to move forward with a positive mindset.

There is a wonderful saying about negative thoughts: nurturing a negative thought is like making a down payment to failure while nourishing positive thoughts is like an investment to achieve success. Negative thoughts are one of the greatest hindrances to achieving the goals we set for ourselves. They can make us doubt our abilities, worth, and purpose.

They throw feelings of discouragement and helplessness at us, making it difficult to stay focused and motivated. When these negative thoughts become persistent and overwhelming, they can steer us away from our purpose and prevent us from reaching our full potential. These toxic thoughts can be insidious, slowly creeping into our minds and taking hold of our thoughts and emotions. We may engage in self-defeating behaviors, such as procrastination, avoidance, and even stepping out from wherever we are. We may become consumed with inadequacy and insecurity, and our self-confidence may take a hit. We may become overwhelmed with fear and anxiety, making it difficult to decide or act.

On the same note, we must learn to recognize and manage our negative thoughts to stay on track and reach our goals. We must challenge these thoughts, ask ourselves if they are true and helpful, and replace them with more positive and empowering ones. And this same approach has helped me throughout my journey. We must be mindful of our thoughts and be intentional about what we focus on. We must take time to practice self-care and nurture our mental and emotional well-being. We must also practice gratitude and remind ourselves of the good in our lives.

As I relive those days of struggle, I am reassured that my family has been my strongest support. They stayed by me throughout this growth, hurdles, and situational transformation journey. Everyone in the family doesn't need to agree with what we say or do; however, as my hair grayed, I realized that family is always the strongest pillar of support anyone can rely upon. In times of joy, they are our biggest cheerleaders, celebrating our successes with unconditional love, and while we grieve, they are the ones who provide us with the strength and courage to keep going.

Within the family circle, we learn our first life lessons and understand the meaning of love and compassion. Without their support, I cannot even imagine where Mathan and I would have been at this point.

Now, since we brought back our online store, we needed experts who could handle the technical tasks flawlessly. While even the most popular organizations fired their employees, Royaloak decided to hire more. While other organizations were taking out their names from job portals, Royaloak provided an opportunity for the best talents in the market. I ensured everyone was happy and content in their new workspace. But when I decided to hire people, my existing team members and relatives asked me whether I had gone crazy. We saw a decline in sales and profit, so everybody thought hiring would be a bad idea. However, as always, I decided to trust my inner voice and move on.

We soon changed our policies and processes for ecommerce platform, built new marketing strategies, and worked day and night on developing the business. Shortly, the online store started taking off; I was neither excited nor worried about it as I knew extreme displays of emotions would be silly. I firmly believe in staying neutral in every situation so that no storm would be strong enough to blow me away. But as soon as the online store started functioning, people started purchasing things. This growth was something that came as a surprise to us even though it was not a huge success.

I wouldn't say we saw a huge sales level because it wasn't that great. However, Royaloak still made a name for itself in the digital world. At first, my team was hesitant to put their faith in the online store, uncertain of how it would fare in the highly competitive world of e-commerce. But, to our amazement, with lots of hard work, it did become a go-to destination for shoppers looking for a wide variety of furniture.

Honestly, it was just an experiment. Although I did not have a negative feeling that it would fail, I also was not sure about its success rate. However, our teammates came up with several doubts: how will we deliver the goods when the government has declared complete lockdown? Will we get payment from our customers without fail? Will they become annoyed if the delivery gets delayed? I did not have a clear answer, but my intuition kept whispering everything would be alright.

The website had been designed to be user-friendly, with a simple and instinctual interface. We also made sure that the products were of the highest quality and that the prices were competitive. Our efforts were eventually paid off. We ensured that orders were processed quickly and that goods were dispatched promptly. This resulted in customer satisfaction, which had, in turn, led to more customers visiting the website. It had taken only a few months for it to become a household name, and we were delighted with the results. But as I said, it was not at all a success. All we got was a trivial amount, which saved the ship from sinking.

Although our digital prominence was surprising, there was a logical explanation. Initially, when the lockdown was declared, people went into a state of shock and discouragement. But as time passed, people had enough time to sit back at home, relax, and spend time with their loved ones. We had no idea about this. We thought people were worried about their lives and taking utmost care of themselves and their families by not leaving their houses. However, it is also a matter of fact that the majority of the world population was facing a state of depression. But at the same time, some people were enthusiastically involved in renovating their little havens with all the possible craft works and accessories, mainly out of desperation and helplessness.

Those were the times when most people discovered their true passion and started working towards it, that too, only due to helplessness. Due to their hectic work schedules, people who couldn't invest time in painting, singing, or dancing hobbies got plenty of time to polish and feed their creativity once again. While one side of the world was focusing on the negative impacts of the virus, there were still people on the other side who were using this time in a way that could change their lives for good. There were people with positive mindsets. They started appreciating the warm feeling of being at home. We did not consider that people might consider decorating their homes. Our only idea was to experiment and see how far it goes. I couldn't make it very popular or generate crores in profit, but we generated a few lakhs, which helped the organization breathe. It helped us escape the financial crunch we had been going through. We were at least able to pay our team well.

Most of our customers were ready to wait for the delivery of the goods they ordered, even if it took one or two months. The cooperation from their end was commendable, and it inspired us to add more products to the online store. As the online store grew, the number of members on the technical wing kept increasing. It was a peculiar situation on the recruitment front. While other companies were busy firing, we were hiring. And this invited several mixed comments and opinions from people around us. Most of them were wondering what made me take this step.

Hiring people takes a lot of financial responsibility. Still, I had my reasons that were sensible enough, a set of reasons that could have a great positive impact on the company and its workforce. Since COVID times were all about unemployment and hardships, youngsters were finding it hard to land a job at a company that could encourage their true potential. We received umpteen applications, and the recruiting team sat and filtered out the best fits for our growing family. The minimum package at Royaloak was handsome enough for any new joinee, and with that, we saw many energetic teammates joining hands to build the company brick by brick.

Even though we multiplied the company's strength by leaps and bounds, one thing was entirely out of our hands- the spread of the virus. Several of our beloved teammates were violently attacked by COVID several times, making them cough and tying them to bed for countless days. When other companies introduced loss of pay for sick leave, Royaloak took responsibility for its team members and provided them with financial and mental support throughout their treatment process.

Living with a positive attitude is great, but surviving after getting tested for COVID-19 positive was the toughest of the battles humans have ever fought in the current century. Every time I got the news that one of my team members tested positive for COVID-19, I felt devastated. It felt like a heavy burden had been placed upon my shoulders, and it was more than I could bear. I knew they might feel like they were in a dark tunnel with no light in sight and surrounded by an overwhelming feeling of despair. They were all so scared and anxious, sometimes making me feel helpless.

My workforce was loaded with questions and uncertainties. Thoughts like "what would happen next?", "would I be able to recover?", "would I be able to return to my normal life?" and many more distressing thoughts ran errands through their minds every other second. Did they come and tell me personally? No. But I was sure about it. Royaloak was genuinely worried about them. I had to take a step back and look at the bigger picture. I assured them that they were not alone in this fight and that I would treat and support them like my family and promised to help them get through this. I had to remain positive and take each day as it came. I was determined to beat this virus and followed all the guidelines and protocols. I urged them to take their medications on time, eat healthy food, and get plenty of rest.

I also asked them to stay connected with their loved ones and people they can find solace talking to. I consider my staff as my biggest asset rather than financial growth. My principle is simple — If the teammates are sick, the company cannot breathe. They are the very foundation of its success. Without them, the gears of progress would grind to a halt. They are the soul of any organization, who keep the wheels of industry turning.

Like a large, sturdy tree, the employees are the company's roots, firmly planted under the ground, providing strength and stability. Their hard work and dedication ensure the continued growth and prosperity of the business.

Without them, Royaloak would be nothing more than a hollow shell, a structure without life or purpose. They are the ones who make it possible for the company to achieve its goals and reach its full potential. I ensured that they received everything they needed at the right time in the right amount and waited patiently until they were completely cured.

When they came back, I never put them under any pressure at work as I knew how difficult it was to get back to work after all the struggles. However, I urged them to practice yoga and meditation as it has helped me deal with many health-related issues, be they mental or physical. Everything was teamwork at our company. My team worked hard, even beyond their key responsibility areas, to bring better results to the organization.

As Hellen Keller rightly said—*Alone we can do so little; together we can do so much.* Teamwork is one of the essential ingredients for the success of any organization. It is like a powerful engine that propels the organization forward.

It is not just about the collective efforts of individuals but also about the mutual trust, respect, and collaboration that make them a true team. The brilliant crew of Royaloak had a mission before them to bring the brand to higher heights of glory. They stepped to the plate as the game began and gave their all. They worked together to ensure victory, each doing their part as an integral cog in the machine. Their skills, experience, and sheer determination were unmatched as they pursued their quest. Every move they made was carefully considered; every action was taken with a genuine purpose.

Even when the odds seemed insurmountable, they never faltered. The team remained focused, and their hard work and dedication eventually paid off. Although the journey was long and arduous, they emerged as winners.

Before the emergence of the pandemic, our store count was fifty-five; after the pandemic, we booked seventy more stores, out of which we could open forty-five stores. With that, we had a total of a hundred stores across India by the end of the pandemic. With our combined effort, Royaloak was brought to a level of fame and respect that it had never witnessed before.

Until the beginning of 2020, we were South India's best furniture firm. But with collective effort and a positive attitude, we became India's topmost brand within a year. The online store was a grand success. The crux of doing business or entrepreneurship is having the courage to take risks with a positive mindset.

Had I withdrawn from my plan of launching the virtual platform under the influence of the negative thoughts whispered into my ears by people, Royaloak would have become a stagnant organization. Or, who knows, it could have vanished into thin air while following the traditional way? Within a short span of time, we signed several property agreements and bought physical stores by conducting virtual tours of the space.

In this era of technological advancement, businesses have been forced to adapt to the changing landscape of the digital world. However, this shift to virtual operations has proven difficult and ultimately unsuccessful for some organizations. These companies have found that the lack of a physical presence has made it hard to remain competitive in the ever-evolving business climate.

Organizations that have failed in this transition to virtual operations have seen a sharp decline in sales and customer engagement. Without direct interaction with customers, these companies have struggled to build trust and loyalty with their clientele. These companies could not effectively keep up with their competitors without the ability to showcase products in person, which had been a cornerstone of their business model.

Furthermore, many of these organizations have found managing employees without a physical presence difficult. Without the ability to meet in person, there has been a lack of unity and collaboration, leading to a decline in productivity and overall morale. This lack of cohesion has made it hard to keep up with the demands of the digital world, resulting in the ultimate failure of these businesses.

My company's success is deeply rooted in my positive attitude and spiritual interest. Applying spiritual principles such as meditation, mindfulness, and self-love has allowed me to stay focused and positive during difficult times and remain mindful of the bigger picture and the higher purpose of my business. Through practicing these principles, I have found my inner strength and courage to face difficult situations requiring me to make firm decisions.

Amid all this, I developed the ability to look beyond the immediate circumstances. I could chalk out a newer perspective with the potential for growth and transformation. Spiritual practices have also helped me cultivate inner peace and contentment, keeping me resilient and focused on the end goals. It has always been the spiritual practices that enabled me to stay connected to my purpose and the higher purpose of my business, allowing me to make decisions that align with this purpose.

I firmly believe that when you focus on the right things, the outcome is bound to be good. As I take a step back and look at the growth of our company, I can't help but reflect on all the hard work, dedication, and strong faith that my team and I have put into the process.

Mathan, my younger brother, has been one of my biggest support systems during all these struggles. He held my hand firmly whenever he felt like I was confused or struggling. Since childhood, Mathan has always been right next to me in everything, whether happiness or sadness.

He took responsibility for the website development and arranged the team for meetings. He spoke to them calmly and made them understand how to deal with certain things. Unsurprisingly, our success has been bolstered by the positive energy and spiritual guidance that we brought together into the office every day.

There were times when I did not know what to do next when COVID hit for the first time. I did not panic or drop my business as I was determined.

We were the first set of people to experience the harsh effects of COVID. People felt stuck in a rut or a loop of unending trouble during the lockdown period. I could have sat in a corner thinking everything was over. But I chose to fight back and rise against what the world feared.

Circumstances might attempt to knock you down. However, you must stay patient and confident because if there is a will, there is a way. If you're meant to win, the crown will naturally reach your head.

Not everyone can make such huge decisions within a short span of time. Courage and self-confidence cannot be built in a day. As a child, I faced many challenges, which eventually made me stronger and more resilient.

Takeaways:

Before Covid-19, Royaloak had just fifty-five stores across the country. However, as soon as the pandemic became less daunting and the government lifted all restrictions, Royaloak experienced remarkable growth, expanding from fifty-five to one hundred stores within a span of less than two years. This journey beautifully shows that every ending is merely the beginning of something new and exciting, filled with endless possibilities and opportunities for growth.

Now, let me take you to my childhood...

"If you look the right way, you can see that the whole world is a garden."
—Frances Hodgson Burnett

Mr. Venugopal (Category head of Royaloak)

Mr. Vijai is a person who keeps all his teammates motivated throughout the day. As part of the team, I can't thank him enough for supporting all of us, especially during COVID. The pandemic's first two to three days were highly confusing; we did not know what to do. Vijai sir held Google and Zoom meetings daily to let us know that we were not alone in this situation. We went on to discuss the new strategies we could implement within the organization during the pandemic outbreak. The only part that helped the company earn revenue was the e-commerce department. For this reason, we decided to prioritize developing e-commerce, and Vijai sir also moved forward to open new showrooms of Royaloak. Vijai sir and Mathan sir, the team leaders, were actively available for their team over calls and virtual meeting platforms.

Every team member willingly worked for the organization from 8 am to 11 pm without hesitation because we were a team and wanted to grow together. To reduce the burden on the squad, the e-commerce branch was split into two sections, and they worked throughout the day to help the company generate income through e-commerce. The rollout team also did a splendid job by virtually visiting sites to launch showrooms, and all this was done with the support and guidance of Mr. Vijai. Everyone was engaged in one way or another, trying to drive the organization to great success.

The best part is that not even a single teammate refused to work despite going through the life-threatening pandemic. We started working early in the morning and continued to work till late in the evening. We saw lots of technical development within the company, and the sales team kept calling customers and clients and maintaining the rapport. So, in general, nobody was looking at the clock. All they looked at was their productivity graph.

Several of our colleagues, including me, tested positive for COVID-19. Some of them had to visit the hospital until they recovered, but many of them stayed back at home and took rest until they felt better. We kept ourselves engaged by working rather than relaxing to distract our minds from the negative outcomes of the virus. Initially, when the lockdown was declared, we were all in a state of panic, but gradually, we realized that it could be controlled or prevented if we could cooperate. In the beginning, we had no clue about what would happen. The initial two to three weeks were a time of uncertainty. We only started feeling better once we returned to work, and all the credit goes to Vijai sir and Mathan sir. They tried their best to keep us active and out of our desperate state of mind. Vijai sir used to say that this is a tough time, and we should overcome this together. He starts his day at work by wishing us a good day. He delivers motivating speeches every morning, and I can say that we managed to survive the situation effortlessly because of that positive energy.

Vijai sir and Mathan sir, as leaders in our organization, have made a significant impact on my professional growth. Observing their approach during procurement has been a valuable learning experience.

Vijai sir's effective deal-closing techniques and Mathan sir's attention to product quality have been particularly insightful. Beyond their business skills, what stands out is their humility and positive attitude, even in challenging situations.

I appreciate the practical lessons on staying grounded and facing complexities with a positive mindset. Overall, the influence of Vijai sir and Mathan sir on my professional development is undeniable, and I'm grateful for the guidance they've provided.

2
MEMORIES THAT COULD NEVER FADE

"The only limit to our realization of tomorrow will be our doubts of today." - Franklin D. Roosevelt

Were you a backbencher whom the class called a non-achiever? Have you ever lived a life of poverty with no electricity or even food for several days in a row?

Have you felt so low that you ended up believing you could not improve your life situation or come out from the mouth of poverty and hardship?

A picturesque village nestled in a valley, framed by rolling hills and lush green meadows; the air filled with the scent of the lovely marigold, the bliss of the petrichor, the chirping of the tiny sparrows, the noise of cycle bells, the little dew drops falling from the tip of the light green leaves! Thevaaram was a village with a breathtaking view of nature.

Beautiful hues of flora and fauna blessed the human life around. The village is in the heart of the Theni district in Tamil Nadu. It has always been a place of tranquility and happiness, and that is what makes it beautiful.

Even though T Ranganathapuram, near Theni, was my birthplace, I lived most of my life amidst Munnar's fragrant wildflowers and tea estates in Kerala. The morning dose of mist with the raw smell of forests is worth every moment of your life. I would trade anything to relive those golden days just to be in the middle of the lush forests.

But was life as picturesque as the nature around? The azure blue sky and the beautiful ambiance around did not hold the same beauty in life. As the saying goes, struggles are for adults, and childhood must be spent without an iota of stress. I was waking up to the thought of finding a new game to play with friends and siblings, roaming around under the sun without holding the fear of anything. Childhood is a phase of innocence and wonders when the world is simpler and filled with a sense of possibility.

It is a time of exploration, discovery, growth, laughter, joy, friendships, and connections. It is a time of naiveté, carefree days full of curiosity and adventure. It is a time of exploration and learning, stories and laughter, discovery and amazement, dreams and hope, comfort, security, love, and belonging.

However, things were a little different for my brother and me. Our childhood was a rugged terrain, fraught with emotional upheavals, often an arduous journey filled with unexpected twists and turns. We navigated through the shadows of adversity, confronting countless obstacles while cultivating our resilience and strength of character.

We literally lived in an underdeveloped place which was nothing less than a jungle. Still, we persevered and emerged as wiser, more compassionate individuals. We lived in a humble abode in the hill station of Munnar, a one-room house without electricity. With the windows overlooking a picturesque landscape of lush rolling hills and the faint scent of tea plantations lingering in the air, we made the most of our simple lifestyle.

Nights were spent watching a million fireflies flicker around in the dark, competing with the stars to cast the most enchanting light show. In the morning, a symphony of exotic birds greeted us with their melodic tunes, ushering in a new day of adventure. Despite the lack of electricity, we treasured every moment spent in the tranquil paradise.

When I was in eighth grade, I was finally able to flip a switch and get an electricity connection at home—walking up to the switch for the first time and turning it on brought with it a feeling of amazement and excitement – the kind that comes with the promise of a bright future.

After years of depending on candles, flashlights, and kerosene lamps to provide light, I could stay up late and easily do my homework. With the addition of electricity, our house felt like a home, and with that feeling came a degree of independence and security.

My brother and I were less fortunate than many kids in the present generation who get everything they ask for. We never had an opportunity even to request our parents to get something done for us.

Bereft of a comfortable place to sleep, many nights were spent counting the stars. Indeed, we lacked a steady source of income or a cozy bed to lay our heads on, but we never complained.

The lack of a soft mattress and fluffy pillows did not dampen our spirits; we accepted our circumstances with a contentment that only came from an appreciation of life's simpler pleasures. My mother had a tiny 'petti-kada,' a tiny stall selling sweets, vegetables, and pickled items.

It wasn't a separate shop on the roadside, but a window of the house we lived in that was extended a bit.

I used to go to Munnar town to handpick each product for my mom's little store. With utmost care, I would shoulder the weight of her beautiful dreams, delicately cradling them as I made my way back home. These trips weren't just about picking up products; they were a heartfelt gesture, each step resonating with love and dedication to fulfilling my mother's aspirations.

It was quite small and could not cover our daily expenses. Despite her best efforts, the profits that she expected were not forthcoming. Her hard work and dedication to the little business had gone unrewarded, leaving her disheartened and deflated. She had put so much faith into this venture, believing it would succeed, but reality took her to a different realm altogether.

Her experience was a harsh lesson for her sons regarding the precarious nature of doing business. I still remember how she kept a firm grip on the zip of her purse strings. It only made us realize how broke she was despite her hard work.

Since then, I have nurtured a dream of rewarding my beautiful mother, who toiled day and night to feed the family. She was, honestly, a tireless worker who dedicated her life to providing for her family. However, despite the long hours and laborious tasks, she never complained.

All I should call it is a show of remarkable strength of character and selflessness. Her unwavering commitment to her family was a source of comfort and security, and we felt immense gratitude and respect for her sacrifices. We wished she could have had a life of more comfort and ease, but she would never have asked for it. We were children; however, we were not naïve or ignorant. My younger brother Mathan and I grew up roaming around the tea estates of Munnar inhaling the raw smell of the lush green tea leaves and we realized we could do a little business by using those tea estates. But we were just kids and had to focus more on academics.

When we moved back to Theni from Munnar when I was around eleven, we lived amidst the luxurious views created by nature. Every time we ran out of money, Mathan and I went to the nearby local places to pluck guavas, the only fruit available there back then. We would stop at the large guava tree in our neighbor's courtyard.

When I say nearest, I'm sure you must be thinking we share the same wall, but no, we had to walk for several minutes to reach their house.

We plucked the juicy, ripened guavas from its branches. Sometimes, we picked up whatever laid on the ground. We filtered the best ones out and often ate some of them, hardly touched by birds or worms. The sun used to glisten off the skin of those beautiful guavas, making them look like jewels. We filled our bags with the sweet fruit and continued along our journey. I still remember how good they tasted. They carried the genuine freshness of nature, devoid of any chemical fertilizer. I could never find such pure organic guavas anywhere in the past fifteen to twenty-five years.

While parting the flesh of the fruit, the juice of it used to ooze out, and it rolled down our fists till our elbows and would then fall on the ground drop by drop, turning the tiny pebbles pink and off-white. This was enough for us to start drooling until it dripped off our jaw. It often stained our already dirty white T-shirts.

Munnar did not have a lot of guava trees, as tea estates ruled the entire town. However, it was still a pleasure for us to roam around in Munnar, enjoying the lovely view and plucking juicy guavas from the trees. The residents of the locality used to like our selection so much that they bought every fruit. It was a different sense of pride while we handed over our earnings to our mother, inexplicable, so much that I could never weave them into words. Then, we were alien to the word entrepreneur. All we knew was to help our mother. Given a chance, I would have named that stage of our life 'kid-entrepreneurship.'

I did my schooling until 6th grade at a local government school in Munnar. I learned to speak Malayalam as Munnar is a popular tourist spot in Kerala. My classmates were mostly Keralites. Being a boy from the southern part of India, I could speak two languages now. Although I was not fluent in Malayalam, I could understand what my teachers and friends said. Tamil and Malayalam have so many similarities in terms of meaning and pronunciation.

Our histories are woven tightly on the premise of beautiful epics and mythologies. We grew up listening to the great Ramayana and Mahabharata stories lying on mom's lap. We were so proud of strong characters like Arjuna and Krishna, who won epic battles and rose to glory, that we badly wished to become someone like them in the future- fierce and fearless.

Initially, it was difficult for me to communicate with the teachers, considering the language and dialect. Still, later on, with their unconditional support and nurturing, I was able to have a beautiful school life. Initially, I used to fail every language test. I still remember the dread that would flood me as I stepped into the classroom, knowing that I had failed my language exam yet again.

Each time the teacher would lower their glasses and sternly call on me to come up to their desk, the smell of disappointment that suddenly filled the air shattered my mind to a million pieces. From the second standard onwards, my father actively participated in my educational journey.

To give me the best possible chance for success and to make me feel comfortable, he discussed with the school principal and decided that I would switch from Malayalam medium to Tamil medium. After sixth grade, we had to move to Theni, where I finished my seventh and eighth grades. Growing up, I was often the odd one out in my class. While my peers seemed to effortlessly absorb the grammar rules of English, Malayalam, and Hindi, I struggled to understand the nuances of these languages as no one ever taught me even the basics of these subjects properly.

I felt constant pressure to keep up and to be able to grasp the concepts as quickly as my classmates, but I couldn't seem to bridge the gap. My grades suffered, and I spent many afternoons poring over books in frustration, struggling to understand everything.

There is a vast difference between the schools and classes in both states. Schools in Tamil Nadu were so crowded that I could hardly walk through the verandas without falling or pushing people to the sides. Kerala was a different story, and thus, it was pretty tricky for me to fix the blocks. Unlike the students of this generation, we never got individual attention from our teachers, nor did we have enough resources to help us learn quickly. Today, when I look at my kids, I see them going through a spoon-fed culture.

They learn everything easily, and everything is readily available to them. Looking back to my childhood, we didn't even have new books to study. They were either borrowed from the senior students or provided by the school. In both cases, several pages were missing; most of the books were torn, all smelled of damp soil and dust with smudged ink from being exposed to water, and with pages where the previous user had scribbled something with different colored pens.

They often had the stains of turmeric due to the carelessness of the previous user. Considering our situation, could I ask for new books from my parents? After all, it is for them that I chose to go to a government school in the first place. I never believed in God, and I hardly went to temples because my mother was the only God for me; for her, I was willing to sacrifice anything and was ready to endure all the pain without complaining.

I had to move from school to school for one reason— our dire financial straits. Our resources were mostly depleted, leaving us with only limited options. The need to make ends meet weighed heavily upon us. We were in a situation that seemed so dire that it seemed impossible to overcome. Sheer desperation ruled our lives. We felt as if we were trapped inside an endless cycle, unable to break free from our financial woes.

We could only hope for a miracle to lift us from our predicament.

However, I believed I could do miracles to pull my family out of this haze of sorrows, just like all the mythological superheroes who had inspired me throughout my childhood.

I shifted to a hostel in Aundippatty in Madurai, Tamil Nadu, at the age of fourteen since education was free there, and I finished my whole schooling until grade twelve there. It was my third school. But this could not be avoided because our financial graph was moving negatively, and we had to cut down on all the extra expenses to survive.

But this time, I was alone. Madurai was hot; however, the essence of the fresh scent of sandalwood coming out of the temples was enticing. I knew this would be my place for the next few years until I finished my schooling. Initially, I was an average student whose progress reports were not colorful with all the plus symbols, but at least there weren't many minus symbols. I spent several days and nights working on the most challenging things, and by the end of grade twelve, I topped the school, not just my class- the boy who struggled to pass his tenth standard just accomplished one of his most challenging goals!

I was never ready to fail; rather, I believed in attempting everything that seemed impossible and proving that everything is possible if one could work hard enough. As Kevin Hart would say, *"At the end of the day, you put all the work in, and eventually, it will pay off. It could be in a year. It could be 30 years. Eventually, your hard work will pay off."* Today, if I am a known name in the market, a huge banner of hard work hangs behind me. Nothing happened overnight. Struggle, penury, sleep-deprived nights, and everything walked with me as a constant companion.

Life is about having the willpower to come out of every situation with a positive result and mindset. Today, when I look at my children, I can see that they tend to refrain from several things due to fear of failure. They are so accustomed to the glory of success that they hardly realize the importance of failure. If the fear of failure prevails, we can never explore anything new. Risk aversion is quite contagious amongst the new generation. They are more comfortable choosing the easier route than struggling to do something new. However, that won't hold right when our country flourishes with new-generation entrepreneurs. As a father, I try my best to keep them motivated every time they think of stepping back. My mantra is—No matter what life puts you through, you grow through it.

While I was living in Madurai, my brother was lucky enough to have lived with my mother back in our hometown under the warmth of her embrace. Penury is often linked with a lack of education. It is like a vicious cycle. People with low incomes don't have enough money for education, and without proper education, one is bound to remain poor.

Even though our financial status was quite miserable, I knew education was extremely important. When several of my schoolmates quit their studies to pursue labor work or get married after schooling, I enrolled in Government College Chittur, Palakkad, in Kerala, to pursue a Bachelor's Degree in Commerce. I did not know much about B. Com, but I was sure that it would help me become the person I wanted to become by helping me craft better ideas for managing a business.

For me, it was like this degree to fetch success while shaping enough knowledge and finesse about running a business. It was like a doorway to a new realm where I could learn, grow, and make life a better place. It opened a plethora of opportunities where I could understand the crucial aspects of running a business.

Although I was not a first bencher, my vision about life was sharper than the class toppers. When most of them just took college as a fun thing, maybe I was the only one in the crowd who never had a glorious boyhood.

When other boys my age were celebrating everything, I struggled to connect the dots. Every day was a new battle with the world, and I had to brace myself well to provide my family with a better lifestyle. Did I complain? Buried by their family's financial worries, young boys often complain about their appalling situation.

Very few like me would rather work hard to seek a solution. Predicting what will happen next is difficult as we are all subject to the whims of fate and the universe. We can never truly be in control of our lives. Therefore, it is important to remember that we should never blame any situation that comes our way. Rather than pointing fingers and assigning blame, we should strive to accept whatever life throws at us.

More than that, we should not let our pride hinder our learning ability. We must grow by grabbing the lessons from our experiences. We should recognize that every situation has something to teach us. We should seek to understand the underlying lessons and use them to become better versions of ourselves. After all, life is not a competition. It would not be very smart to compare our experiences to those of others. Everyone's journey is unique, blending success and failure, glory and struggle, and peace and prosperity. Instead of sitting and pondering upon what others have and what we haven't, we should strive to be the best version of ourselves and focus on our progress. Let us be grateful for the challenges we face, for they only shape our success story at a later stage.

My childhood or family was not all about poverty and struggles. Mathan, a few lovely cousins, and I shared an unbreakable bond. We were more like friends than cousins. Everything around us had always been about adventure. When kids of the twenty-first century played with Xbox and PlayStation, we played with fishing wires and sometimes even snakes. Senthil, one of our favorite cousins, often mentions that all those fantastic memories still feel alive when he closes his eyes.

We used to swim through the crystal-clear waters of the nearby rivers and lakes and throw pebbles into the waters to see the ripples form. Ah! It was a pleasure to have lived through such splendid moments that time could neither erase nor recreate. Every time we spend family time together, Senthil walks us back to all those memories with a pleasant smile.

As we grew older, Senthil moved to Singapore to pursue a better career. He was a part of our mango-plucking team. He used to join us at the nearby local places and helped us select the best mangoes to sell at the stores. How could I even forget those splendid memories? I wish life could give me another chance or a time machine to travel to those days to experience and cherish those few best moments of life. Of course, I don't want that hardship to hover around anymore; however, the taste of the sweet memories is unforgettable. Although I do not remember how I used to be as a boy, according to Senthil, I was a very serious and tough guy with a profound vision of becoming an entrepreneur someday.

He saw me as a person of solemnity and gravity, measured and tempered yet passionate. He would say that I was a person of solemn reflection and contemplation and deep thought who could go beyond the surface to discover a world of meaning beneath.

Mathan, on the other hand, was quite a contrasting character: bubbly and effervescent, always eager to engage in lively conversations. He was an incorrigible charmer, able to light up a room with his liveliness. His playful nature was infectious, and it was impossible to stay aloof for long around him. He was a talkative little boy who used to climb trees and play with insects. While I was analytical, Mathan was the epitome of spontaneity; his enthusiasm for life was contagious, and his impulsive nature was often a source of joy and amusement.

We were a vibrant group of nine cousins: six boys and three girls. Every year, for all the festivals and special occasions, we would get together and sleep on the floor, making memories that would last a lifetime. We were all so different but shared a bond like none other. We rarely got to see each other, but it was like a house on fire when we did.

During those good times together, we would run around chasing chameleons and wild elephants, our laughter ringing. We created stories and played games, and our imaginations ran wildly around the thick forests. We would all sit in a circle, talking, sharing stories and secrets, giggling, and listening to each other. Every year, we made a promise to each other to meet the following year again. We did our best to keep the promise.

We vowed never to forget our promise to each other and strived to keep our word, dreaming of the days we would reunite. While saying goodbyes, our eyes used to get filled with tears, knowing that the time we spent together was special and fleeting. But the memories and the bond we shared stayed with us forever. In the years that passed, no matter how much our lives changed, we were always there for each other. Those days were the best part of my life amidst all the worries and responsibilities on my shoulders.

It is a matter of fact that life was never a bed of roses for our family. The roofs leaked during the rains and drenched the room. Monsoons are a nightmare to the people in Munnar even today. The entire route is well known for its hairpin passes, which are quite dangerous.

While most of the kids in the present generation spend their weekends at pubs or bars or home binge-watching series, we spent our weekends going into the forest area, crossing the passes to collect wood to burn the hearth to prepare food. We had to be very careful. The roads had water and pits on either side that even a little inattention could take our lives. But unfortunately, we had no other option.

In the rugged terrain of Munnar, where nature held sway with its erratic weather, Mathan and I forged our unbreakable bond. Our childhood was no stroll through a sun-dappled meadow; it was a ten-kilometer trek from home to school, each step a testament to our determination. Munnar's climate was a marvel, a symphony of extremes. Rain cascaded for six months, followed by a scorching sun that ruled for three, only to yield to a winter's icy embrace. Our path was no well-paved road; it wound through the hilly, mountainous terrain, a testament to our resilience.

Umbrellas were a luxury; if one was found, it became a lifeline against the deluge, leaving the other to brave the downpour. As raindrops danced around us, sweat cascaded down our determined faces, a fusion of effort and adversity.

The culmination of our journey, arriving at school, was a victory etched in our young hearts. It symbolized a refusal to surrender, an indomitable spirit that even the harshest elements couldn't quell.

Home was a sanctuary, a single-bedroom haven that bore witness to our humble beginnings. There were no modern conveniences; the hiss of an LPG connection was foreign to our ears. Instead, weekends, as I said earlier, were dedicated to foraging the forests, gathering wood like provident squirrels, stockpiling against the inevitable monsoon.

With foreheads glistening with exertion and legs that wobbled with fatigue, we climbed trees and hacked away at branches, fueled by a determination to secure our family's fortune.

Those trying days were the crucible that forged us, shaping us into the resilient souls we are today.

The trials we weathered in our youth have paved the way for the blessings we now embrace.

Our lives have found stability, a testament to the power of grit and the unwavering belief that hardships are but stepping stones to a brighter tomorrow.

My mother kept saying back then that everything would change for us one day. But none of us were able to see it coming any soon.

How far could it even be? I've thought about this for myself almost every day. But sitting and thinking about the things that you don't have is never a solution to the situation that lies ahead.

If there is anything that could change the present, one needs a positive mindset. One must have the courage and nerve to take a risky leap.

My father was not as supportive as my mother, and that was another big misfortune we faced while growing up. Though his presence was a comfort, his lack of monetary support was a constant source of strain. His contribution to the household was not enough to sustain us, leaving us to rely on our resources for financial stability.

Our lives were a balancing act, with each of us contributing to the family's well-being, but his absence in this regard was always noticed. We had to be creative in chalking out different modes to make ends meet with meal plans, budgeting, and stretching out even a single rupee as far as possible. We all felt the weight of his shortcomings realistically, having to stretch ourselves to make up for what he couldn't provide.

Coming up with every possible solution to make the most of our limited resources and to ensure that the family was not starving was an arduous task. Even though we had a spirit, it was still essential to have a method to commute. When the rest of our cousins lived moderately luxuriously, we felt like outcasts. When they had brand new cycles and motorcycles, we were here walking and tiring our tiny legs. We never wished for anything new or fresh. We never wanted everything, just something that could make us look better.

When other kids slept under comfortable roofs, we slept under our mother's hug, which was the safest place we had ever slept in. Although Amma's 'petti kada' was not highly profitable, everything displayed got sold out on time on most days. But then, there are days when not even half of the stock gets over.

We pulled her closer to us and consoled her every time. We promised her every time that one day we would make her feel proud of us and that one day we would all have nice clothes to wear and not the old clothes of our elder cousins.

Ah! Those were the days. We struggled, but we never let the smile fade away. We had our share of worries; the prevailing plight sometimes seemed unpalatable. However, as we ran our errands under the sun, we kept gathering experiences. A popular saying is that doing business is not everyone's cup of tea. This is possibly true because one must be willing to work harder and harder to make their business plan work.

My childhood was indeed quite different from my friend circle and, of course, difficult. However, as I relive those beautiful memories, I realize that I was probably born to do something great, and the supreme force was chiseling my abilities right from the beginning. Childhood memories have a significant influence on our growth and mindset. A happy childhood does flourish into better adulthood. So, was I unhappy as a child? Bereft of many luxuries of life, I had witnessed hardship. Certainly, I was not the happiest child; however, I had my share of joyous moments. Plucking the mangoes, helping my mother run the household, running random errands with my brother, and everything had shaped different, beautiful memories for me.

Somehow, my brother and I continued to move ahead with faith. Being positive and not complaining has taken us so far in life. We were ready to appreciate even the most trivial things we had. However, we were only surviving rather than living. At this point,

Mathan and I realized that we had to find a permanent solution to the situation. We were never ready to give up ever. We might be born poor, but we were sure that we would never die poor. We fixed in our mind that we would improve our situations together and have a better life. If I could become the school topper coming from a place where I did not even know how to write in English well, why can't I become the leader of my own life and pull my family from the well of starvation? As Walt Disney rightly said, *"All our dreams can come true if we have the courage to pursue them."*

Takeaways:

The life we carved out amidst the wilderness only served to fortify me with each passing day. I learned never to cast blame on my circumstances, for every twist and turn in life ultimately unveils unexpected treasures beyond our prayers. The strength I attained from this jungle life is what strengthened my road towards my entrepreneurial journey.

Senthil (one of Vijai's cousins)

Vijai has been quite a smart person since childhood, or I would rather say he is still a sharp and steady young man. Another thing that makes Vijai perfect is that he is highly focused and hardworking. He clearly knows what he wants and does everything he can to achieve his target, no matter how trivial it is. Vijai is five years younger than me. He always tried to stand out from the crowd. All the abilities he possessed were unique. He was and still is exceptionally artistic. He used to draw pictures that looked so realistic; I haven't seen a person as creative as Vijai. He is more interested in doing things that people would not normally do as he always wanted to be different from everybody else, even from me. Vijai was a bit of a serious person compared to Mathan, whereas Mathan was a naughty child who kept climbing trees, chasing chameleons, and running around all the time. However, neither of the kids was a trouble to anybody. Vijai had a difficult childhood as he had to jump from school to school to different locations in Tamil Nadu and Kerala. It apparently had affected his academics, making him an average student. Although not academically outstanding, he was pretty active in other activities like painting and drawing and maintained his focus on the things that he liked to do. He was not into sports and other extracurricular activities in school since he is a reserved person, or rather, I would say, an introvert. He is a totally different person now. He is no longer an introvert and has started liking socializing. He used to withdraw himself from talking to people in public, but now I feel really proud of the person that he has become: a man who would willingly speak to everybody without hesitance.

After finishing his bachelor's in commerce, Vijai actively started searching for a job. He was keen to experiment with something new, and I remember he used to like buying things and selling them for profit. With this attitude, I was sure that he would become an entrepreneur one day. The only person from our family who ran a business was Vijai's mother. I believe that Vijai took inspiration from her during his early boyhood. He attempted to do many things for profit, starting from the tea powder business and everything else that followed. He used to go to the nearby farms and pluck coconuts and mangoes and sell them at the local shops in the area. This was in the 1990s. I was settled in Bangalore and was working as a civil engineer at a construction company. I used to live in a small apartment in the BYG building in Balepette, Karnataka. I always wished that both Mathan and Vijai could come to Bangalore, but they were still in college back then. But I knew that they were planning to host exhibitions in different parts of the south to earn something for survival. They soon stepped out and began to sell tiny plastic articles and exhibition halls in Kerala and Tamil Nadu, and eventually, they came to Bangalore as well. They managed to pool up some funds and bought a secondhand scooter and traveled miles on the scooter to buy the products that had to be kept at the exhibitions. Before he realized that TV stands were his thing, he used to sell things like burners and other home décor products, and that too for hardly five or ten rupees. They spent weeks selling their goods completely and kept traveling as much as they could to expand their little business.

I was not personally involved in any of Vijai's exhibitions as I was occupied with my site work in Bangalore. However, I knew that things had started to work out well for my brothers. I guess the first store in Bangalore where they exhibited their products was in Safina Plaza, which was almost close to Prestige Infopark, my office on MG Road. He had to face several downs in his life during this era, but he picked himself up from where he fell. He is a courageous young man and knows when, where, and how to make the right decision in life. Starting from Safina Plaza, Vijai saw steady growth in his career.

The doors of my apartment were always open for Vijai and Mathan every time they visited Bangalore. But I could not have so much fun with them as I moved to Singapore in 1995. Although I was not there, my brother and our other cousins used to stay there. It was a great shelter for everyone in the family. I think Vijai first started off his company with the address of my apartment in

NO MONEY? NO PROBLEM!

Balepette.

Vijai spent most of his childhood in a village in Munnar in Kerala. We met only during festivals, that too hardly once every year, but all our cousins used to be there to make the most out of the time we had. Together, we used to visit temples, bathe in ponds, and have so much fun. Talking about the cousins, we were six boys and three girls. Vijai's father is younger than my father. My father is the second son, and Vijai's father is the fourth one, so I was one of the eldest cousins Vijai and Mathan had. We stayed together in a small house that did not have the space to occupy all of us. Little did we worry about what we didn't have; we spread a mat on the floor and slept there like clothes packed inside a carton.

Since it was a village, we were blessed with breathtaking views of nature all around. There were places that resembled jungles, and there were small streams. We used to walk through the borders of those tiny streams, balancing ourselves from falling into the water. We caught fish from the stream and even got onto boats that were tied on the shore. There were deep wells that were dangerous, but we still walked around them. We used to climb mountains and hills, plucking blueberries and chasing chameleons and elephants, and Mathan, the naughtiest of all, sometimes caught snakes and ran through the entire village. I, being the eldest in the generation, was the person in charge of the safety of my young little cousins. We knew hundreds of folk songs and kept singing them as we walked through the boundaries of forests and hills. During one festival season, I cannot recollect the year we went out to do all our crazy things, but this time, we took our cousin sisters along with us. I will never forget that day. We created some beautiful memories and reached back home after around four to five hours. All we saw was my father standing on the veranda with a stick bigger than my size. Being the eldest child in the gang can sometimes be a curse because I got beaten up by my father so badly for taking the kids out without informing anyone and coming back late. The little ones escaped from the scene quicker than the wind. So, ultimately, we did crazy and wild things throughout our entire childhood.

Our grandfather passed away when I was in eleventh grade, and Vijai was studying at a school in Aundipatty, which is Tamil Nadu. Although he attended the funeral, he was stuck in his hostel when the whole family was traveling to Rameshwaram to perform our grandfather's final rituals. We had booked a bus, and fifty of our relatives were inside. I was finding it really difficult to travel without Vijai. Even though he was a silent person, his presence is something that brings so much positivity to everyone's mind. I asked the driver to stop the bus near Vijai's hostel in Aundipatty, and we picked him up from there so that he could also join us on the trip. The moment Vijai boarded the bus, we started singing and dancing, causing trouble to our aunts and uncles, deafening their ears with our screams and shouts. We even forgot that we were on the way to pour out our grandfather's ashes; we made it look more like a picnic. Can Vijai even forget this? I don't think so.

We created tons of memories as kids and even as adults. I returned to Bangalore from Singapore in 2005. In the meantime, Vijai had almost created a safer space for himself and his business in Bangalore and had started to earn well. After I returned from Singapore, we used to hang out and party a lot. We went on trips to resorts predominantly in the Mysore region. It was never a boys' trip but rather a family gathering. We used to book resorts inside forests for two or three and stayed there. One fine day, while staying at a beautiful resort in Vythiri, we decided to go out into the wild to chase elephants; how could the inner adventurous child inside us even go away? Our families who accompanied us said that they wanted to see what an elephant looked like from a closer point. Well, we said okay and started walking deeper into the forest. One of my best friends, Suresh, was also there with us that day. The deeper we went into the forest, the more it began to look haunted, and within another few minutes, we happened to see a herd of elephants, but the scariest part was that they were preparing to chase us. With all the life we were left with, we ran zigzag through the forests with our wives and children. We thought we were about to be killed, but with the grace of god, we managed to run out of the forest to a safer place. This was one hell of an experience and can never ever be forgotten.

We gather once every two or three months and enjoy to the hilt. Sometimes, we dance until three in the morning, but we never get tired of it. Apart from all the fun, Vijai is a hard worker. He enjoys everything, but the very next day, he gets up and steps out for work. I haven't seen a person like him in my entire life. I have been living a corporate life for the past thirty-five years, but not even once was I able to be a person like Vijay, who is very punctual and disciplined. He wakes up at 3:30 am every day; not even soldiers would be as disciplined and obedient as Vijai. I have worked for the Ministry of Defense, but even then, I could never adopt Vijai's qualities. Vijai works to improve his business from 4 am in the morning to 9 pm at night, that is, for all seven days a week. When people take a day off on Sunday, what Vijai does is plan what to do on Monday. He is a person who is living evidence of the fact that consistency is the key. We used to go on long drives on some days. What people normally discuss on such fun drives would be about spending a vacation or finding a nice restaurant for lunch, but what Vijai does is ask me about how corporate structures work. He has always been a good student. He tried to learn new things every single day. I never got tired of explaining to him how my industry works. I worked as a project manager for a corporate company where popular IT firms like Google and Facebook were our clients. I had to travel across the Middle East and Asia as I was the operation director representing India. Vijai showed great interest in listening to my growth stories. He constantly kept asking me about how I managed to earn such a huge designation and how I managed to travel overseas to grow in my career. He even used to ask questions like how to identify good people or a good HR, or I would rather say he was keen to know how I managed all the operations and stuff and how things were implemented. He tried to learn how to prepare presentations and present them confidently. The best part is he applied all the lessons he learned in his own entrepreneurial life, and I am more than proud to say that he did things better than others who have experience in the same field. Unlike others, he listened to everything and stored it inside his brain rather than forgetting about it the very next hour. He does a lot of homework and seeks expert advice before he implements anything. The consistency he maintains in whatever he does is what makes him the best.

It was in 2019 that Vijai started thinking about expanding his business and making it a franchisee business, and this was the time when my parents fell sick, which eventually made me leave Singapore. I had to settle in India to take care of my parents. But unfortunately, within a year, the novel coronavirus took the entire planet for granted, and every industry had to see a downward graph. I couldn't travel back to Singapore since airlines shut down for several months. I decided to start a business and work on it so that I could make an identity for myself in India. Even though businesses worldwide saw a decline, Vijai was the only person who made a difference. He did exceptionally well. People were firing employees, but Vijai concentrated on hiring more. This was when he asked to invest in his franchise. His store in Erode was taken up by Vijai and one of my friends named Ghuhan, while I took charge of the other store at Karur. Another store at Dindigul was taken up by me and one of our cousins from Dubai. Since Theni was Vijai's birthplace, he wanted a franchisee to be there, and I took charge of that store. I was in charge of three franchise stores in total. The business did not go well in the initial few days, and I told Vijai that I didn't feel this was a promising one. But Vijai was not deterred or discouraged by what I expressed. The only thing he said was that his intuition was leading him in the right direction and that everything would work out soon. I believed him because I knew that Vijai would always find a way out. Within a few more months, everything changed as Vijai promised, and the destiny of Royaloak changed commendably. My life was also changed, and I realized that joining hands with Vijai was such a positive thing I had done in my entire life. Soon, Royaloak grew to become South India's number-one furniture brand.

I would take forever to finish talking about Vjiai, or else I would have to write another book about him. It is hard to believe that he grew from zero to a billionaire within just twenty years. People tend to give up when they see things are not going well, but Vijai's consistency and determination are what took him to where he is right at this point. He is a person who is deeply into spirituality; he is a person who embraces all the doubts and uncertainties within himself every single day before going to the office. He follows a lot of Sadhus (saints) who teach how to perform yoga in the right manner. Believing in sadhus does not mean we believe in human beings who impersonate gods. It is just that we believe in the power of meditation. We used to do yoga and meditation for hours and hours in wild places like on top of the hills or in the middle of forests, and even on the banks of rivers and lakes. Vijai still does that; he meditates for forty to fifty minutes every day, but I cannot even imagine waking up as early as 3:30 am like Vijai to meditate. We strongly believe that meditation helps in controlling emotions such as anger and anxiety and helps us become more focused on other important aspects of life. Deep-rooted spirituality is one secret of Vijai's entrepreneurial success. Even though I am his elder brother, I have learned a lot about success, focus, and ambitions from him, and I'm yet to learn many more things from him, like discipline and obedience.

3
BREWING SUCCESS THROUGH HARD WORK AND CONSISTENCY

"If opportunity doesn't knock, build a door."
- Milton Berle

Imagine you were planning to become a young entrepreneur, and all of a sudden, an angel appeared in front of you, holding in hand a magical wand with a whirl that your life could change forever. Would you let that Angel create the magic, or would you turn them down to live your life adhering to your own terms and conditions?

There is no right time to do something that has the capacity to change your entire life; there is no right time or age for a person to decide whether or not to become an entrepreneur. I thought about it at an age as early as eleven as I wanted to make my mother happy. I was determined to make a name for myself, and I was willing to put in the hard work and dedication to make it happen. But I never knew where to begin.

However, I could not afford to witness my family struggling. Living an unstable life and moving from state to state came with its own challenges; adapting to the climate, balancing finances, and earning for everyday meals were quite arduous. Life certainly gives you the opportunity to run away from it, but do you think life would still make sense if you did not dare to face a situation? Challenges are given to fighters, and losers keep losing the battle every single day. Mathan and I were warriors.

We were ready to walk through roads of fire and back without giving a second thought about the burns and pain. That is what deprivation does to you. You become exceptionally courageous because you have nothing to lose.

Rich people worry about losing money, but people like us only have to worry about our lives. Penury has the ability to snatch away your sleep, your peace of mind, and your everything, only to leave you empty-handed for an uncountable number of days. It can be seen as a source of resilience, a catalyst for the courage to face the challenges of life.

It can imbue a person with a formidable strength of character and resourcefulness, enabling them to persevere in the face of adversity. In the face of hardship, poverty can bring out a tenacity of spirit and a deep-rooted determination to survive and ultimately thrive. While going through all the downs, we were grateful for what we had. When you look around, you get to see people who live in even worse conditions.

Do you want to know what it actually was like for people in our neighborhood? Life was hard and hollow, empty and rough for them. They had no home to call their own, no food to fill their belly, no hope for better days ahead, just a life of misery.

So many went without the basics, their children's needs were ignored, and they lived in a constant state of fear with no one to lend a hand.

We were fortunate as we had enough to keep our bellies at least half filled every day. Even though our roofs leaked, we were happy with it, for our neighbors never even had a roof. So why bother about the leaks? When you look above you, you may find people who live under better circumstances, which might leave you in a state of jealousy and dissatisfaction, but the more you look at people below and around you, the more you find the inspiration to live. You find reasons to feel blessed rather than cursed. Embracing everything makes you capable of achieving better things.

It is all about being positive and confident during the onset of tragedies and misfortunes. After all, like I always say, everything is just temporary. Like they say, "This too shall pass."

In the heart of a scenic village called Chittur, in the Palakkad district of Kerala, a new chapter in my life unfolded as I embarked on a journey of higher education at Government College, Chittur. But unfortunately, the college never had its own hostel.

The prospect of a hostel outside the college loomed, an additional expense I couldn't sidestep. Yet, it was a challenge I embraced wholeheartedly. Balancing studies with the art of cooking became my daily ritual, leaving little room for leisure.

However, I was unable to manage my expenses. Mom's unwavering support manifested in a little money; she placed two thousand rupees into my hand, a lifeline that tugged at my heart, which was still not enough.

Taking money from her was a heavy burden, knowing the depths of her own struggles. It was then that I resolved to forge my path through a venture - a tea powder business. From the verdant hills of Munnar, I sourced the tea, undertaking the arduous journey to Chittur.

When I came up with this thought, my mother unhesitatingly handed me two thousand rupees, which she had been saving for several months. Although it was an act of kindness, I was upset about the fact that she would have to struggle for several months to bring her life back on track.

Dividing the bounty into manageable parcels, I sought out local vendors in Chittur village. Yet, adversity struck. The unbranded packets met skepticism; the absence of a recognizable label caused a stumbling block. Again, monsoons were a nightmare. Rain-soaked packages tainted my effort, the rich aroma of the decoction seeping through the bags and staining my resolve. This affected one of my consignments. Undeterred, I pivoted towards Kochi, navigating the bustling auction scene to secure quality tea at wholesale prices.

I had a conversation with a dealer who helped me out by providing the best quality tea powder. I opted for ABT parcel service to whisk the product away to Chittur, liberating myself from the hassle of dealing with stubborn decoction stains. I combined the small packets and converted them to packets of half and one kilogram each. The shift was transformative. Shopkeepers and hotel owners in Chittur welcomed the rebranded product with open arms. Soon, I opened a small distribution unit.

Since the moment I shifted to Palakkad, Mathan was so alone at home that he did not have a companion to fight and have fun with. He felt so lonely without me, like a bird with a broken wing, unable to fly.

I could see his sorrow in his eyes, and it pierced my own heart. I missed his presence, too, but there was nothing I could do. We had to go our separate ways. However, I made sure to keep in touch with him as much as possible.

At certain stages in life, there is no point in holding on to emotions and staying back. Leaving your house and relocating to a different place may sound scary and heartbreaking. But sometimes, that becomes a necessary change that the heart craves without even us knowing. Life can become tough, and that is the same in everyone's story. Nobody could write about a hundred percent happy life. There would not be a single person on this earth who has never cried in their entire life. I made my brother understand this fact. He was initially finding it difficult to digest.

After all, he was too young for a philosophical awakening. But he was never ignorant. He never walked away from the advice of people who were older than him. Or I would rather say it was never about the age of the person who gave the advice that he respected, but the depth of the sense it made. He could have made his childhood a splendid one by running around, plucking mangoes, and throwing pebbles into the rivers. But he never did that. He never spent his time lazing around and playing with his friends.

The first year of college whizzed by like a fleeting breeze, leaving me hungry for both academic excellence and business expansion. I wanted to prepare for my second-year exams. That's when I turned to my steadfast ally, Mathan. His love for me knew no bounds, and he readily shouldered the responsibility of the business, allowing me to bury myself in books under the dull yellow bulb.

He continued to visit the estate, purchasing tea packets, wrapping them neatly, and selling them to the same old fancy hotels and tea shops in Chittur village. Well, when I say fancy, it does not mean a setup like Starbucks or CCD. For us, the tiniest tea shops, which sometimes had a thatched roof or maybe even more than one bench in front of it, were luxury. People do have different definitions for the same thing.

For some of you, luxury can be having a mansion, a chef to cook your favorite food, a car to help you commute, or truckloads of money to purchase anything under the sky; but for my family and me, being able to afford dinner for four people for three consecutive days was the best definition of luxury.

Mathan, despite being way too young than me, was a very sensible child. I have always been proud of the little boy he was- imagine having the spirit to take forward a business that too without a push from any older people! He was everything that I have always wanted to become- childish and playful, yet serious and ambitious, and moreover, courageous.

Post-exams, I eagerly plunged back into work, fueled by a newfound ambition. Together, we pooled resources and acquired our prized possession – a secondhand bicycle. It seemed like a far-fetched dream, but we were determined to make it happen. After weeks of scrimping and saving, we finally had enough money to buy it, and we couldn't believe our luck.

We were so proud of ourselves for achieving something that seemed impossible just a few weeks ago. We took the cycle for a spin around the block, feeling like kings. It was more like we could achieve the impossible.

Despite undergoing hard times, we managed to make our dreams come true. But the best part was the feeling of hope that our little vehicle gave us.

We suddenly felt like anything was possible. We weren't limited by our circumstances and were capable of making our own way in the world. It may have been a secondhand cycle, but it was our symbol of hope. Well, I knew this was just the beginning.

Being the rulers of our kingdom, we flew through the wind like dandelions, but deep inside, we constantly thought about how to change things around us and live a better life. Eventually, as the business blossomed, our mode of transport upgraded to a handsome Chetak scooter.

Days kept moving, and several dawns and dusks passed by. I could manage to afford my daily expenses. But still, our family life looked paused. No significant progress was happening; no huge profit was gained. We went on to discuss a way to develop the tea powder business in the best possible way.

Having an idea is great, but what is difficult is building a strategy to make it successful. However, my family was really happy and supportive. They were happy to see that I kept my efforts consistent to make things work.

Although I relied mainly on parcel services, I often traveled hundreds of kilometers from Palakkad to Kochi to collect the packages myself to build my tiny empire step by step. The bags were too heavy to carry, but anyway, they were not just bags but bags full of dreams and hopes. I somehow managed to load them into the KSRTC bus successfully every time. If you have ever been to Kerala, you will know what it is like to travel by public transport.

I was always a lover of the window seats, for they had a lot of beauty to offer. The wind was like a gentle caress, tenderly stroking my face as I sat on the bus. It was like a kiss from my mother, reassuring me that all was well in the world. Everywhere I looked, I saw beauty. The blue sky stretched out above me in an infinite expanse, dotted here and there by fluffy white clouds. The sun shone brightly, its golden rays casting a warm, comforting light on the landscape. The trees swayed in the wind, their branches reaching out to me, inviting me to pause and appreciate the peaceful beauty of nature. The wind carried with it the scent of freshly cut grass and wildflowers, a reminder of the beauty of the world around me.

I closed my eyes and listened to the soft whistle of the wind in my ears, the sound seeping into my very soul. I was filled with a sense of calm and contentment, a feeling that everything was just as it should be. The wind was like a friend, a companion on my journey. I felt its embrace, guiding me along the path, carrying me gently toward my destination. I felt protected and loved, aware that I was part of something much greater than myself.

I opened my eyes and looked out of the window only to see the glory of the universe. Every time the wind swayed, my wet, dark brown hair was combed backward, and with that, I felt like I was an actor. I was still in my teenage years, and of course, I lived a bit in a fantasy world of movies, too.

I pretended to close my eyes and imagined becoming rich, getting married, building a house, gifting my mother something nice on her birthday, and so much more, just like how Rajinikanth and Kamal Haasan used to do in their movies. Rajinikanth's role in the movie "Bhaasha" was indeed an inspiration. A person who hardly managed to feed his family by driving an auto turns into a popular gangster who stands up for the ones in need, and people start calling him "Baasha." What a movie it was! You could become anything you want to. The situations you were born into have no control over your future because the future is something you create and is not a predestined thing that will eventually come to you while you sleep inside the comfort of your room. If an auto driver could become the hero of Mumbai, why can't a child entrepreneur become a strong and influential billion-dollar business owner in the future?

The bus kept moving through the road, jumping into every gutter that was on the road, splashing water onto the people who walked on either side of the road. Every now and then, I kept opening the bag underneath the seat to take a look at the beautiful packets to reassure myself that everything was safe, and not even one of them jumped out of the bag when the bus passed a speed breaker.

As soon as I reached Palakkad, I jumped out of the bus carrying my bag of hopes and walked towards the hostel to sort the packets to make them easy to sell. I made friends with a local Palakkadan (a resident of the Palakkad district) who lent me a helping hand whenever I was confused about anything related to sales. He was truly a nice guy and was totally happy to help me with everything he could. While continuing to sell tea packets at tea shops, I came across an exhibition that was happening in Palakkad. This was a new thing, and I badly wanted to give it a shot.

I've been to watch exhibitions with my uncles before, and this time, as a young adult, I wanted to experience it from a different perspective, which obviously is not to stare at the giant wheels but to do something that could help me earn something. I had no idea about what product to display, but I still wanted to participate. It was a sure thing that selling tea powders there would make no sense. I started researching what could be done and went to the stalls to enquire about the money that I had to pay.

They fixed an amount that was a bit beyond what I was expecting. But I knew that I was one more step closer to the person I wanted to become. Without a second thought, I arranged the funds to pay the rent at the stall and acquired a space. However, I was still puzzled about what to sell.

Palakkad is a bit of a dry place to find products that can be sold from a business perspective, but there are still thirteen more districts that can offer something great.

To begin with, I traveled to Kochi since it is considerably closer to Palakkad. Kochi is a tourist spot even today, with a touch of French quality everywhere. I roamed through the streets of Fort Kochi and came across a wholesale apparel shop. Plenty of colorful clothes were hanging on the walls as well as folded and kept on racks. I made up my mind to purchase them and sell them at the new stall.

We may not know what is going to work out the best for us. It is only through experiments that you figure out what you are born for. Finding the purpose of life is a tough task, as it takes uncountable trials and errors. If you fail an attempt, never assume that life has come to a dead end; it could be a lesson; take a closer look, please. You would only feel better. But the uncertainty of life can jump into the picture anytime and anywhere with bitter outcomes. It is never under our control, nor can it be foreseen.

Things were not working out well. People didn't even turn to a piece of garment to see the quality or to check the color and size. I was pretty close to plaguing my mind with intensely sorrowful thoughts. But in the next second, I realized that apparels were a bad idea and not the last idea. The world is a wider canvas, and you can paint pictures with several colors. I realized this could be just one color that would not blend well with the picture that I was painting.

However, I decided to try my best until the stock was over, but unfortunately, the exhibition came to an abrupt end without notice as the owner of the entire setup had other plans for himself. I was left in a state of despair.

What do I even do with these many clothes? What would I do to cover up the loss? I was in a puzzled state. But, as I said, there are many more colors that are waiting in the queue to be explored. This was the first biggest financial loss I had experienced. I somehow managed to distribute the clothes among my friends and relatives. Some of them paid for the product, but most of them were interested in considering it as a free gift rather than considering it the helplessness of a broke young entrepreneur. I had to return to the hostel with a heavy heart and an empty pocket.

While stuffing the clothes back into the bags, tiny droplets of sweat were rolling down my hair to the forehead like pearls, only to hit the eyebrows and gently move to the sides, following the curve and falling on the edge of the plastic sacks and take a little bounce and splatter like raindrops on a window grill. I was sure that my eyes were sparkling with the salinity of the tears that were standing near the cornea, waiting to break out as soon as I gave it a slight blink. I convinced myself by saying, "This is not the end of the world. There are more things that are crying in the corner and waiting for your attention; explore them. It might help you reach the place you want to." Your inner voice and your intuitions have the power to take you to the peak of Everest, which may sound technically impossible to the world.

In the meantime, my tea powder business started to reward me with trivial amounts of profit. That was my source of income to afford my college expenses. Government colleges are not as exorbitant as private ones, and for that reason, I never had to spend even a single penny on my tuition fees. Accommodation and food were the two main things that demanded monetary involvement. For me, it was not easy, but still not impossible, to have an income to fulfill these necessary requirements.

For my classmates, three years of college life were all about fun and entertainment. While they went to movies and shows, I stayed back at my hostel to arrange the packets that had to be sold the next morning. My room used to smell like tea. When normal people woke up to bed coffee and bed tea, I literally woke up to the fragrance of those fresh tea leaves, and that felt even better than drinking an actual cup of tea. I maintained self-discipline that my melatonin alarm, with its invisible hands, lifted my eyelids open every morning at 3.30 am. I arrange all the books and stationeries every day before going to bed so that there is no need to rush in the morning. Government College Chittur was an amazing institute amidst the slanting pine trees and thick and tall oak trees, which we sometimes called the grandma tree as they were older than the college. The entrance of the college had a huge arch made using bricks with the name of the college engraved on it in dark metal black color.

The building was painted in yellow, making it look like a typical government college, which it actually is. The surroundings were like a garden full of *Mimosa pudica* plants, which are also known as shame plants and touch-me-not. I was always in love with the sight of how easily its pretty leaves slept like a baby with just a light pat. Looking at them for another few seconds until they woke up used to give me a rare form of hope- it is okay to take some rest for a while, but in the end, you are surely going to wake up stronger than before. After taking a look at all the beautiful views around me, I went to the classroom, and I am proud to say that I haven't bunked out so many lectures like the rest of my classmates. But, even before the classes started, I got up and went to the shops along with the friends I made there.

He held one bag in one hand, and his other hand kept swinging back and forth as we walked through the tiny, muddy roads of the villages.

While the tea business kept going on just fine, a hotel owner in Palakkad saw potential in me and offered me the opportunity of a lifetime. Was he an angel? The promise of change hung in the air. The horizon seemed to stretch infinitely, promising a future shaped by determination and daring dreams.

   I knew that opportunities like this would never knock twice. With all the excitement of becoming a hotel owner, I sealed the deal with an advance of Rs. 10,000/-. I couldn't help but be deliriously happy about this big achievement. My mother looked at me with her lovely eyes filled with tears of joy. After all, her son did everything to keep the family together and bought the hotel by saving every single rupee without even eating or drinking for several days.

There were days when I skipped breakfast and lunch as I couldn't reach back on time in the morning after distributing the packets, and sometimes, I deliberately skipped them to save money. However, in the end, it started to feel like all the hardships finally started paying off. Mathan was even more excited to be a part of the hotel and was willingly waiting for his chance to stay with me.

Our Chetak scooter, at this point in time, turned out to be a great relief. It was an asset. Mathan sat at the back seat of the scooter, holding tight onto my shoulder and screaming out loud as we went on a mini ride through the outskirts of our locality. You get to realize the beauty of life once you start achieving everything you want, one by one. The family's destiny was about to change, with this hotel in Palakkad being our source of income and status in society. It is a matter of fact that working hard and being kind and optimistic will lead you forward in the direction of success.

As the quote goes, *"Work hard in silence; let success be your noise,"* I worked for this moment since childhood, and by the beginning of adulthood, the story of my success was almost prepared to make the noise. But the unforeseen future had something else in its treasury waiting for me. I was imagining doing everything I could to make the hotel a popular one in the town and shifting my family from Munnar to Palakkad to show them that Palakkad is nothing less than Munnar. I wished to send Mathan to the same college where I studied if he liked that idea.

What would I name my hotel? Should I name it after my mother, or should I consider our family name? What color do I paint the walls? I was confused. However, I had to concentrate on academics equally, and for that, I found time to skim through my textbooks even early in the morning and at night before retiring to bed.

No matter how busy I was, I knew that a graduation certificate was extremely important for me to survive in this beautiful world, even if the hotel business failed by any chance. A formal education was the only backup plan I have ever had in my entire life. Everything else was based on intuitions. Trusting the process is yet another vital point. Come what may, be prepared to deal with it in a calm and gentle demeanor.

I was planning to move to a nicer house or room which would be sufficient to accommodate the four of us- a house with strong walls and roof, a nice kitchen, a clean washroom, and a nice hall where we could sit and chat in the evenings with a cup of tea and some snacks brought from our restaurant.

Every preparation to hasten the process of opening the restaurant was going on in full swing. I was happy that I was about to do something significant at the young age of just twenty-one. However, like everybody else's story, mine was also overwhelmed with a miasma of unanticipated misshapes.

Just weeks before the opening of our family's dream venture, my uncle came into the picture, holding a golden ticket to a destination I had never dreamed of before, just like an angel with a magic wand. I was left in a quizzical state of mind. I couldn't turn him down, nor could I give up on myself.

What could I even do? Being a person who is forever prepared to deal with all the sudden attacks and confusion, I decided to wait and see what the future had in store for me. However, deep inside, I was curious to know what would happen next. After all, like Joseph Campbell once said, "*We must let go of the life we have planned so as to accept the one that is waiting for us.*"

Takeaway:

If you aspire to succeed in life, the foremost requirement is the willingness to exert efforts towards your dreams. Having no money is not even a problem as long as you are willing to put efforts. Simply remain steadfast in your determination, and forge ahead to execute your plans.

Mrs. Janaki Subramaniam (Vijai's Mother)

He is a soft and silent person who never creates a nuisance or disturbance to anybody around him. He was a calm person who performed really well in his academics as well.

He has always wanted to become an entrepreneur. The business was always there at the back of his head. All our relatives and friends were well settled in their lives; they either had well-paid jobs or owned a business and were leading a moderately luxurious lifestyle, but ours was not in a good state. Vijai badly wanted to help us out.

Although I come from a wealthy family, my father misused the funds and used them for other unnecessary purposes, which eventually led the entire family to a state of destitution. Vijai knew about all this and wished to earn well enough to improve our situation and bring it back to how it once used to be, and he started contributing towards this dream ever since his college days. I have been a housewife all my life, but I badly wanted to do something for the family, which is why I opened a petti shop in our locality. I guess Vijai also got a bit inspired by my little initiative. I also think both Vijai and Mathan have adopted several of my qualities in their lives. I wouldn't say I like the idea of wasting time. I have never spent a day in my life loitering around and being unproductive. I value every single minute and use it wisely, unlike other women who sit at home doing nothing. Vijai might have felt that I was worried about several things, especially financial issues, which could be one reason why he decided to step into the field of business.

He was very good at school. He studied at Little Flower School, Munnar, but they only had classes up to the seventh standard. We had to apply for both Vijai's and Mathan's transfer certificates once Vijai completed his upper primary school. But at the same time, Mathan had one more year to study in the same school, and for that reason, they refused to issue Mathan's transfer certificate. As a matter of fact, 'Little Flowers' was the only good school in Munnar, and the principal genuinely wanted us to let Mathan continue there for one more year as they were concerned about his future. We finally decided to send both of them to Tamil Nadu, only after which the principal of Little Flower agreed to issue the transfer certificate for Mathan. I still remember and can feel the warmth in their principal's tone. She requested us to send them to the best school in Tamil Nadu because she was so sure that these kids had a bright future ahead. Vijai was way too different from other kids of his age. When the rest of them played and had fun in their free time, Vijai used his time to do something creative and useful. He used to make dolls and statues of eminent personalities like Mahatma Gandhi and Indira Gandhi out of clay and mud. We were shocked to see this kind of flawless work coming out of a little boy. He paid attention to detail because those tiny little statues had the prettiest eyes, realistic hair, sharp noses, structured jawlines, and infectious smiles. He used cotton to make Indira Gandhi's hair because she had light gray, curly hair. We used to feel surprised. For Gandhi's statue, he ensured that his spectacles looked realistic, and for that, he used steel wires and bent them with great effort to make them into a circular shape. He used to draw very well. Although he is really quiet in nature, he has a sharp personality inside.

Talking about the relationship between my two sons, Mathan always obeys Vijai. He never does anything beyond Vijai's advice and instruction. Mathan never talks back to him, and Vijai's decision is the final one in everything. They have never parted ways, no matter what happened. They have always stayed close to each other, and that's how I raised them, too.

When Vijai started doing the tea powder business, he packed it all by himself and kept those packets only inside his room. But unfortunately, it did not take off much. I don't know where he went wrong, but it was a partial failure; it might have happened that way because that wasn't his destiny. He never spoke about this incident, nor did he share the pain he was feeling with me, thinking that I would become sad and disappointed. When we sent him to Palakkad for higher studies, I wasn't aware that his first exhibition business was a failure. I was only expecting him to study well. He never told me about his feelings. He managed it all alone and never did anything that would hurt me.

When he told me he wished to move to Singapore, I really wasn't happy about it. I did not want my children to go away from home. Our kids should always be with us. Also, I believe for a person to be successful, what is important is hard work, and for this reason, I didn't find any justifiable purpose in his going to Singapore to make a living. I was totally against the idea of working under an organization. I wanted Vijai to stand on his own feet without being controlled by an upper layer of management.

When Vijai moved to Coimbatore, the only way we got in touch was via handwritten letters. He worked in a bank in the marketing section and had to work quite hard to earn something for survival. But still, my son, with his first salary, gifted me a gold ring, and I felt so proud of my child. I don't even know how to put this feeling into words. Not everybody would get kids like Vijai and Mathan. I feel so blessed and lucky to be known as their mother. They are really responsible and caring people.

When Mathan and Vijai opened their stores in Bangalore, we, as parents, gave them mental support. However, the business strategies and other marketing ideas came from Vijai. Mathan followed everything as instructed by Vijai. I always remind Vijai that Mathan is his biggest strength. I raised them in a way that they would never stop obeying and learning from each other. The strength of their bond is something that I cannot describe. It is so deep that they both chose their life partners from the same family so that they could stay together forever.

Royaloak was not at all popular when Vijai opened the first store, but today, the entire family is known by the name of the brand. Even when we attended a funeral a while ago, I heard people from the crowd talking about us, addressing us as the Royaloak people/family. That is the kind of power we possess at this point. Hearing this from the general public makes me feel so proud of my children.

If you ask me about a memory of Vijai that I still remember, there is this one painful thing I would talk about. One day, when he was a little boy, he came home running from a distance holding his head, and the moment I lifted his hand and moved it away, I saw blood flowing out from the wound my son had on his forehead. I will never forget that day in my life. Vijai is a calm child who never got into fights and arguments with other kids, which kept me wondering how he got injured so badly. Upon interrogating for a while, Vijai confessed that he was hit by a bully child in his gang. But Vijai did not want to hurt him back. If it were Mathan in Vijai's stand, he would've hit him back because he never lets people blame him without a legitimate reason. He never lets anybody hurt his elder brother or parents. Even today, after their marriage, they still take care of us the same way they used to do before marriage.

I want them to be happy and successful wherever they are. I want us to be together and face every hurdle together. When I look at Mathan and Vijai, I can see how well they have stayed true to the meaning of brotherhood and proved that love and affection are more important than money, especially in this Indian culture and context where people run behind wealth and possessions.

4

A SINGAPORE NIGHTMARE: SURVIVING DESPITE ALL THE SETBACKS

"A goal is not always meant to be reached. It often serves simply as something to aim at."
– Bruce Lee.

Have you ever faced betrayal from a person whom you have admired all your life? You must have been heartbroken, weren't you?

With each passing day, I was getting one step closer to my long-term dream of becoming an entrepreneur. My intention was never to reap a profit of millions of dollars in cash but to be capable of supporting my family, feeding them every meal, and helping my brother complete his studies.

After paying the advance for my dream venture, I shifted from Chittur municipality to the middle of Palakkad in order to run the business in full swing. I stayed in an area called Kalmandapam in a rented house named Ashraf Manzil. It was not really spacious; however, that was all that I could have afforded at that point in life, and I was always grateful for what I had. Moving to a space where the roof didn't leak anymore made me feel as if I was in a beautiful mansion; it appeared luxurious to my eyes. I made friends with the drivers and conductors who lived next door. They, too, were in a rat race to make ends meet, no different from me.

When hard times grab you by the collar, you should have the courage to confront them; never run away. The hotel was about to open in a week. Everything was moving ahead in a way better than I expected. Moving to a better house was indeed an achievement. That was when a huge twist occurred in our lives, which gave us the hope to dream bigger. My heart was filled with joy when my beloved uncle from Coimbatore journeyed to our humble town to spend time with me and my family. I was overcome with emotion and anticipation, as I couldn't wait to reconnect with him and hear the stories he was going to share.

We talked late into the night, sharing stories that weaved together like a beautiful tapestry of our lives. I was so grateful to have him near and to be able to share in his incredible life experiences. He was my mother's younger brother, who was not just an uncle but a role model to us. When our family was drowning in a dearth of basic needs, he imparted intense courage to us and sometimes helped us with financial support. He has even gifted us kids so many clothes. Even if they were oversized, we loved to wear them only because they came from him. Walking up and down the hills holding his hands is something that I will never forget.

No matter how many friends we make or how far we venture from home, our families will remain to be the best part of our lives. Our families are our pillars, who will always be there to provide us with love, support, and understanding. They would love to stay with us through every step of our journey, from our first days of life to our last.

It is a fact that they have seen us through our greatest triumphs and our most heartbreaking defeats but still remain our greatest source of comfort, strength, and joy. It is a bond like no other, a connection that transcends time and place. It is a love that will never fade and a legacy that will be passed down for generations to come.

Our uncle was one such humble personality in our family whom we loved so much.

His visit to Palakkad had a beautiful intention that kept me motivated to have daydreams- he wanted to whisk me away to the exotic shores of Singapore, a place of beauty and awe, where I could explore a new culture, a new world. We would wander the streets, hand in hand, exploring the vibrant markets and rich history of this vibrant land.

I could almost feel the warmth of the sun and the excitement of a new adventure dancing on my skin. I could imagine the sounds of the city and the delicious aromas of its cuisine, tantalizing my taste buds. The thought of it filled me with a deep longing for something more, something new and something special. Until that day, I had never imagined boarding a flight and traveling abroad. When airplanes flew past our hometown, I used to think how fortunate the people sitting inside the plane would be. The innocence of children is something that makes them think outside of the box. They may think running after a flying airplane will take them to a different country.

Mathan and I were also like that. We were filled with a sense of awe and wonder as we watched the planes soar above us, their wings slicing through the sky. We were entranced by the beauty of the moment, feeling as if the whole world had been paused and we were the only ones in it.

We followed the planes with our eyes, unable to look away until the clouds swallowed them up, and they disappeared from our sight. In that moment, we felt a deep longing to take flight and explore the world, to break away from the monotony of our everyday lives.

When my uncle came with the news of taking me to Singapore, so many thoughts rushed into my head like a swarm of bees that broke out upon being disturbed. How do I continue my hotel business? Won't my parents have to live in Munnar again for another few years until I get settled? How would Mathan feel? Won't we miss each other? I couldn't stop thinking. But none of my thoughts had negativity; they were all reasonable questions.

My uncle always wanted the best for his nephew, and therefore, I trusted him so much, which eventually made me say yes to him; I don't get too excited no matter what a person says. Even if I win a jackpot, I would be calm because life can change within seconds, and there is no point in being sad or happy for a moment. After all, as Birbal advised Akbar, *"This too shall pass."* Even the deepest sorrow you face today is impermanent.

My uncle believed that living in Palakkad would make me weak as I grew up, and my family would not have all the fortunes that they deserved. I decided to obey him because I knew that he was trying to help us out. When my uncle informed my parents about this huge step, they began to weave their dreams of having a better lifestyle. Mathan was over cloud nine. He couldn't wait for me to leave so that in a few years, he could also join me, and together, we could have a good time in Singapore. Being a young little boy, he was way too eager to get new clothes imported from Singapore, along with chocolates and other gadgets. That is how teenagers behave. I was already twenty-one, but he was not even eighteen. To me, he was still a kid back then. Even today, when he comes to me for an opinion, I stare at him for a while only to wonder how much he has grown up in all these years.

On witnessing the happiness of the family, I couldn't say no to this opportunity. Together, they broke all the earthen money banks at home, counted the money, and handed it directly to me without hesitation. It was then that I realized how badly they wanted me to go and bring back happiness to the family. I always knew that, at the end of everything, my family would be the only people to hold my hands, walk me through the tough times, and keep me from falling.

My mother handed me over a bundle of currencies and coins, which was altogether rupees five thousand. She pledged her favorite pair of earrings and arranged seven thousand rupees more, making it a contribution of a total of twelve thousand rupees. This still was not sufficient to afford the ticket, visa, and living expenses in Singapore. I pledged my scooter for another seven thousand rupees and was almost set to travel to Chennai to carry out further procedures of the trip.

Before that, I went to Palakkad to bid adieu to the hotel to which I had paid the advance amount. That day, even if the weight of the tea powder bags was absent, I felt a weight all over my body and heart. I couldn't stop thinking of how I looked under the seats to confirm that my bags were safe. Everything was different this time. I don't even remember if I was happy. I would rather say I was numb about it. The last time I traveled to Palakkad, I was confused about what to name the hotel I was about to own, but this time, I was on my way to put down the shutter and close the hotel chapter forever.

It was part of a dream, but destiny had different goals. No matter how meticulously we plan, our lives do not always follow the trajectory we have set for them. Fate often intervenes unexpectedly and sends us on paths that we had not anticipated. It can be unpredictable, and sometimes, despite our best efforts, our best-laid plans can be thwarted.

When this happens, we can feel frustrated and confused, as if our efforts have been wasted. We may become discouraged and think that our dreams are impossible. But it is important to remember that fate can be our ally, not our enemy. We may be surprised by the new path our lives take, and we may have to adjust our expectations. But these unexpected turns can lead us to wonderful experiences and opportunities that we would never have encountered otherwise.

If we can learn to embrace these changes, we can find joy and satisfaction in the unexpected. Rather than seeing a deviation from our plans as a failure, we can learn to look at it as a chance to discover something new and explore unexplored possibilities. By letting go of our expectations, we can open ourselves up to the wonders of the unknown. We may still plan for the future, but we should also be prepared to accept whatever path fate places before us.

Just a few days before I left home, my little brother Mathan came to me and said he would terribly miss me.

What did I even do to be blessed with such an amazing brother? We were always like the sun and moon. Our relationship was built on understanding and deep mutual respect. We were both unique in our own ways, but somehow, we connected - like two puzzle pieces that fit together perfectly. We were always there for each other, no matter what.

We shared a level of trust and comfort that was incomparable. Together, we laughed, and we cried, we shared stories and secrets, and we made memories that would last a lifetime. We never had to say it in words to know how much we meant to each other; it was written in the air between us.

No matter how much time passed, our bond never weakened. We were connected in a way that transcended time and space. To this day, no matter what, I know I can always rely on my little brother. He will always be a part of me, just as I am a part of him.

In a few days, my uncle booked my tickets to Chennai, and I left home with a heavy heart. We took a room and stayed in T-Nagar in Chennai. My uncle's love was like a warm blanket, enveloping us in a cocoon of security and care.

Yet, beneath this loving embrace, I could feel the shackles of his addiction to alcohol. It seemed like an ever-present shadow, looming over the family like a dark cloud.

Even in his moments of tenderness, there was a sorrowful undercurrent that made me painfully aware of how much his alcoholism had taken away from his life and how much it was affecting the people around him.

The love I felt for him was sometimes tinged with sadness and a heavy understanding of how much he had become lost in the world of alcohol and its booze.

Once he is drunk, he'd be in his own little world, completely oblivious to the world around him. It made me sad. I wished he could find another way to relax and unwind after a long day, but he seemed to be addicted to the booze. I'd seen him suffer the after-effects of his drinking, too. He'd be moody and grumpy the next day, and he often had to miss work due to the hangovers. I tried to talk to him about it on more than one occasion, but he shrugged it off and said he knew how to control himself. I wished he could see how his drinking was affecting his life, but I knew it wasn't my place to push the matter. All I could do was be there for him and hope he would eventually realize what he was doing to himself. He used to live in Coimbatore, and Mathan and I have traveled to Coimbatore from Munnar to meet him twice. Both times, we witnessed him abusing alcohol. My uncle was a troubled soul, and I knew it. His life was filled with sorrow and pain that he rarely spoke of, but I could see it in his eyes. Even though he had alcoholism, he was still a caring and loving person who never failed to show his affection. He used to take us out to the parks and exhibitions, and he would always offer to buy us treats. He treated my younger brother and me as if we were his own sons and as if he were our adopted father. He was always there for us, and he was the one we could always rely on. When we were down, he was the one who would make us laugh. He was the one to tell us stories and teach us lessons, the one to take us on long walks and show us the beauty of the world, and the one to provide us with warmth and comfort when we were scared. But most of all, he was the one to remind us that we were loved. He was the one to show us that we were never alone. We always wanted to see him as a person who was completely out of his alcoholic behavior, but that never happened.

We reached Chennai, but day one was not as good as I expected. However, I was ready to wait patiently for that life-changing moment. Uncle brought a friend of his to our room, and I saw them sitting there in the middle of the hall and drinking alcohol from dawn to dusk. Uncle beckoned me several times and asked me to buy fried chicken from the restaurant downstairs so that they would have something to munch on along with the drinks. I literally had to work as a delivery person without remuneration for him.

The next day, the number of drunkards in the house increased. This kept on increasing day by day. It was getting difficult for me as this event started occurring as an episode for four consecutive days, and my finances were getting drained. I managed to tolerate this torture only because I loved him so much and never wanted to offend him. But once things started growing worse, I had to stand up for myself. One afternoon, I gathered the courage to let him know how annoyed I was. My pitch was a bit higher than usual, and within no time, everything went out of my hands as my tone provoked him so much. I couldn't forgive myself for having yelled at him at the top of my lungs out of frustration. The anger that welled up inside him, in addition to the influence of the drinks, worsened the situation, and my uncle was forced to kick me out of his place.

My only intention was to make him realize how disturbing it was for me to spend the money on drinks. Every single penny I had with me was the blood and sweat of everyone at my home, including my brother. I was in a state of despair. I could neither go back nor do I have enough funds to survive in a city like Chennai. I was afraid to face my mother as I hurt her brother and had already spent half of the money she gave me by trusting both of us. My parents were not really willing to send me to Singapore as they wanted their children to be with them always. However, we had to have a better life, and for that reason, they hesitantly agreed to let me go.

I couldn't help but weep the whole night at a local bus station in Chennai. The salty tears kept streaming down my face like a river of anguish. I felt a weight on my chest like a boulder of emotion crushing me. I felt so helpless, so sorrowful, and so lost. The tears continued to pour as if they were never-ending. I looked up to the sky, searching for a sign of comfort, but nothing was there. I searched within myself, hoping to find an answer, but nothing was there as well. I felt so alone and so broken. People were staring at me. A man crying was a shame back then. They might have assumed that I was a light-hearted person who was weak enough to fall with the hit of a slight wind. Only I knew what it felt like to have lost every hope and not know what to do next.

With all the money that I was left with, I took a bus to Coimbatore and took up a tiny space for rent to sleep. I cried my heart out in the absence of people and lights under the darkness of the night—a day passed by in an ocean of tears. The next day, I couldn't get up from the floor because I had not had proper food for several days. But still, I knew that life walks you through hell to make you stronger than everybody else. I wished several times that I could go back to have some rice porridge prepared by Amma, but I was constantly worried about how she would feel about my behavior towards my uncle.

Anyway, I did not want to starve myself to death, so I gathered all the spirit I could and went downstairs in search of food, where I saw a few people laughing and enjoying their lunch. For a moment, I thought of talking to them. Without any hesitance and out of the convulsion to rescue myself from the edge of a breakdown, I confronted those people and asked if they could help me find a

job.

They stared at me for a while as if I was from a different planet. One of them scanned me head to toe and came one step forward. I was curious to know what he was going to say – "Come and meet me first thing in the morning tomorrow," said the stranger. Not even for a moment was I scared to go and meet a stranger at a place where he summoned me. The world is a dangerous place. Even people you really know could take you to strange places and rob you or threaten you to do something against the law. But at that point, I was not even concerned about anything. There was not even a penny in my pocket to be robbed.

The next morning, as discussed, I went to visit him at his place. To my surprise, he offered me a job in a leading international bank at that time as a salesboy. I was assigned to sell credit cards to people, and they promised me a salary of rupees one thousand seven hundred. I knew this was not enough since the rent itself would consume six hundred rupees from my account. However, this was my only ray of hope for quite some time. With the money I had, I brought my scooter to Coimbatore since the sales job demanded an active mode of commuting. I was able to sell seventy cards in the first month, whereas the rest of my colleagues were hardly able to sell twenty-five of them—this developed room for an ego clash. I had already become the worm on their career ladder. In the second month, I sold more than hundred cards, and in the third month, I sold more than two hundred of them.

The best thing about this job was that they provided incentives for each card sold. The manager kept comparing others with me, and this escalated the level of their rage toward me. My colleagues were seething with envy, like a dormant fire that had been suddenly stoked.

As soon as they saw that I was out-earning them, they descended like a pack of wild animals, determined to drag me down. Their beady eyes followed my every move, assessing, measuring, and noting down any missteps.

I tried my best to ignore them and focus on my work, but I could feel their anger and resentment like a thick fog that hung around me. I knew they were jealous of my success, and they wanted me to fail.

The person who brought me to the company couldn't stand that I was climbing up the ladder of achievements. So, he, along with a few other colleagues, forcefully took me to the basement of the building and beat me up until I bled. I had only seen and heard of such incidents in movies, and I never expected that this would happen in real life. They asked me to quit and leave the town.

Tears rolled down my cheeks uncontrollably. It felt as if life was taking me to a strange and haunted place where I could never survive, a place where I didn't belong to. I went straight to my manager and narrated the whole incident to him. He apologized for the whole event and took this issue forward to the head office in RS Puram, following which the branch manager appointed me at their head office.

I was not too excited about this. After all, my ex-colleagues were still after me. However, I was confident that I would survive this situation somehow. With the newly gained enthusiasm, I continued to increase the company's profit by leaps and bounds. Even though everything was working out just fine at this point, I had an inner feeling that this was not how I wanted my life to be. The salary was not sufficient to meet the needs of my family.

If I couldn't repay them for their love, why do I even have to work? By this time, although Mathan was already working in a local shop in Munnar, he wasn't really able to take the responsibility of the entire family on his shoulders. I knew it was my responsibility to support him as a big brother.

Working for an organization until my back broke and not receiving enough pay for the hard work started to bother me so much that I started thinking of resigning from my job. Since then, I have kept on making plans to develop my own business and become a complete entrepreneur. It was not easy. But I knew that *"what is meant to be will always be."* Making the right decision at the right time is the ultimate recipe for a successful life. All you have to do is remain positive and trust the process because, in the end, life is never going to push you into a pit forcefully.

If it were somebody else, they would have given up on life the moment they got hit by some random strangers in a basement. I got a chance to be at the head office only because I was ready to wait patiently to see what life had in store for me. Success never happens in an instant; rather, it is a result of constant effort and patience blended with hard work and determination.

Keeping your mind devoid of all negative thoughts will let you see the pit for yourself, and it is you who decide whether or not to fall into it. For me, being stuck in a town with thousands of anonymous faces and not knowing what to do was definitely one of the toughest situations. Had I not spoken to the stranger who later became my colleague, I would have fallen into the deepest trench and would have struggled to pull myself out of it.

It is always about taking risks and showing courage. If not, everyone would be tied to the dungeon of life where you could do nothing but live blind in the dark with the false belief that is where you belong.

We might have set our foot forward for a cause, but life takes us through a new track totally unrelated to the cause. However, you have to stay positive, take risks, and embrace everything with a positive outlook and not in a pessimistic way. Everything happens at the right time.

What my father now says is that he is happy that the Singapore thing didn't work out at all, as he thinks I would have ended up being an employee for some MNC there. He is proud of the person that his son has become after all these years of hard work.

I had already made up my mind to quit the job and pursue a different career. After several days of contemplating, I could finally think about something that would most probably change our lives in a better way. I was not worried about its success rate, but I was ready to give it a try. What I learned within that time period was that facing a betrayal is not the end of the world because if one person leaves your life, there will always be a vacant space for opportunities to come and knock. I was so ready to experiment with new things. Like someone once said, *"Life is about taking chances, trying new things, having fun, making mistakes, and learning from them."*

Takeaway:

Every failure takes you one step closer to success and every no takes you closer to a bigger yes. Never give up halfway. Keep fighting until you reach your goal.

Mr. Subramaniam (Vijai's Father)

My son has always been the biggest support to the family, ever since his childhood. He was a very calm little boy who never gave trouble to any one of us. As he grew up and moved to Palakkad for higher studies, I asked him to concentrate on his academics. But he was highly ambitious and wanted to do some business. He wished to become an entrepreneur. But I forbade him from doing it. I was only expecting him to study well. I did not support his idea back then. I suggested he forget about it until he graduated. But Vijai told me not to worry and that he would handle it well. He promised to put all the effort into making it succeed. Unfortunately, the first exhibition business he did turned out to be a failure, but he never let me know about it. He took responsibility for the loss and never informed me about the challenging situation; nobody knew about the hardships and pain he had gone through. I was totally unaware of it since I was already against his idea. But to be honest, I've always admired the way my son has been handling things. Even today, I admire the way he deals with his customers and vendors, the way he sells and markets his products and all that. I sometimes forget the fact that I had once forbade him from following his passion because he was doing his job as if he was born to do it and had been doing it flawlessly all these years. I keep observing his activities. His marketing skill is unbeatable; he keeps talking until the customer agrees to purchase. He is very good at convincing people and getting his work done. When I say he is good at selling his products, let me also make one thing clear- Vijai sells only the best quality products. He never keeps a low-quality thing inside any of his stores, and the customer would never regret purchasing it. I'm absolutely proud of him and the way he works.

After his graduation, he got an opportunity to move to Singapore, but unfortunately, things went downhill for some reason. But today, at this point, I feel it is good that it never happened because had he gone to Singapore that day, Royaloak wouldn't have happened at all. Back then, people used to go to Singapore with a tourist visa, but finding a job as a BCom graduate would have been difficult for my son. We went to the collector's office to obtain an official letter from them and collected every sort of document for him to move to Singapore. The last thing the embassy asked was for an offer letter from somebody who works at a reputed company in Singapore. At that point, I approached my brother and requested that he provide an offer letter for Vijai, but for some reason, he refused to do so. That incident disappointed me to the core that I tore apart and threw away all the letters and documents that Vijai had received earlier and walked away from the room in exasperation. But as I already said, I'm glad that we didn't send him to Singapore, or else he would've been working as a staff in some organization there. Look at him today - he is the owner of a company; what a proud moment for a father! During the times when all these events were happening, I realized the fact that, sometimes, the people whom we consider as our closest families tend to become the biggest mistakes of our life.

However, I think he is an amazing and highly talented young man. When his business started to excel, he traveled to China to import some international furniture to the Indian market. When he told us that he had a plan to visit China, I did not let him down or forbid him from doing so because, by that time, I had realized that I must trust my son. I really don't interfere much because I'm confident that my son would only do what is best.

His journey from Oak and Oak to Royaloak is the result of his hard work and sweat. My son never prayed for wealth or a luxurious life. All he wanted was to have a life free from poverty, and for that reason, I would say it's all the outcome of his uphill battle. He always keeps an eye on the ongoing trends in the market and ensures that his stores are filled with the newest arrivals rather than what people are already bored of seeing and using. He is fearless and never bothered about the outcomes of certain risks; the only thing he says is that the future of a business is always unpredictable, what is meant to happen will happen, and all we have to do is to be equipped with all the methods to deal with the situation.

Both my sons, Vijai and Mathan, take good care of us. He takes my wife and me to five-star restaurants and treats us really well. Every day spent with them is a beautiful memory. One thing that I dislike about both of them is that they control my food intake. They want me to stay healthy and live long, and for that, they literally stop me from eating things that I like. Well, when thinking from their point of view, whatever they are doing is right; they want me to be fit and fine, and it is indeed a blessing to have children like them who care about their parents.

The more they grew up, the more our relationship shifted from parent and children to friends. We share everything with each other. They take us out for long drives and trips to different places. They have gifted us a number of moments which made us feel so proud of them. One such incident is still bright in my memory. They gifted me a new blazer, pants, and suit and set up an event, something like a success party. They invited me and my wife to the stage and honored us in front of all the guests. They made us feel so special, and I will never forget that day. I still have that suit and pants with me in my wardrobe, and for me, it is a symbol of my children's love and respect, and yes, it is also a symbol of our pride and joy.

I'm so proud of them, and I think I'm truly lucky and blessed to be known as their father rather than them being known as my sons. If you ask me what the secret behind Vijai's success is, I would say the first thing is his character. It is only because of his good character and his courage to move forward that Royaloak is standing where it is right now. The second thing is his behavior towards his workforce. A happy and satisfied team member would undoubtedly ensure that the company is growing and that Vijai and Mathan are indeed their favorite people and their role models equally. Vijai's courage has only increased with each passing day, and that is another factor that drives him to success.

Viaji is never worried about the failures that might come his way because he is confident that his enthusiasm and positive way of thinking are more powerful than anything in the world. It's amazing to witness the level of his courage increasing every day. He assures us that everything ends only in success. I feel very content in life today, and when it comes to my grandchildren, it is beautiful to see how well they have been raised.

If you can be honest and committed to what you are doing, you will definitely succeed one day, and Vijai is a person who has proved that it is true.

5

THE EXHIBITION TRIUMPH: A PATH TO TRANSFORMATION

"Don't be afraid of change. You may lose something good, but you may gain something even better."
— Unknown

Does your gut say you must come out of where you are at right now? Do you think you deserve better than what you already have?

Once you realize your true potential, you must never settle for anything less. Working under an authority is equal to putting yourself under a difficult or sometimes even disrespectful circumstance. Or I would say that it is like deliberately placing your spine under someone's boot to be crushed. I had never imagined that my presence at the bank would call for tough competition or that it would ruin my relationship with my colleagues to the extent that they would show the nerve to hit me up. There was an urgency to get out of this situation somehow. I was tired of roaming around through the city, capturing high-profile people and requesting or sometimes even begging them to buy a credit card. One day, as I was returning home from work, I happened to come across a government exhibition complex. It took me straight to a beautiful flashback from my childhood. As a kid, I was so attracted to giant wheels and roller coasters at exhibition centers that I used to force my uncle to take me wherever it was happening.

As a part of my craving to explore myself and my capabilities, I decided to become a part of the exhibition stall in Coimbatore. But unlike other businesspeople, I never had an idea about what product to sell, nor did I know what kind of products had the highest chance of survival or could reap the highest profit in the market. I was not sure if there were any vacant stalls as well. However, I couldn't refrain from giving it a try. I walked through the area and checked out what everybody was selling, which was when I noticed one empty stall. I was curious to know if I could take that area for rent and sell some exciting products. I went to the inquiry desk at the corner of the complex and asked him for the details about that one empty stand. It was as if that stall was attracting me so much that I couldn't resist not enquiring about its availability. But the rent amount left me open-mouthed for a while. They said I had to pay rupees twenty-eight thousand to have it for a month.

How do I even pay that much? The salary I received was literally peanuts compared to the expenses I had, and with that, how is it even possible to pay twenty-eight thousand rupees? I knew this was quite unaffordable; however, spirituality was the foremost thing that led me forward. I kept my mind devoid of negative thoughts. I trusted my instincts the most, knowing they could take me to places.

I did not want to contemplate further that I said yes to this opportunity. I paid the team an advance of two thousand rupees and walked back to my room with the power of an entrepreneur who took the first step toward his dream. What meaning would our existence even have if we lacked confidence and trust in ourselves?

The next step was to arrange the money. Making twenty-six thousand more appeared to be a herculean task, but I was never planning to step back from it. After all, I knew that a little hard work would definitely pay off. I got in touch with two of my friends,

Santhosh and Karthik, and asked if they were interested in being a part of this experiment, and they were more than happy to join hands with me. And once again, for the second time, I had to pledge my scooter for eight thousand rupees. Along with another ten thousand rupees that I had saved, I had a total of eighteen thousand in my pocket.

This time, once again, I was confused regarding what to display. The Palakkad exhibition gave me nightmares. However, I did not want those memories to haunt me and push me away from my goal. Though one attempt may have failed, it does not mean that all attempts shall be in vain. Hope, like a beacon of light, remains in our hearts to keep us striving for what we desire. Even in the face of adversity, we must not give up, for the possibilities of success are infinite.

I had to make a decision soon, as the preparations for the event were happening in full swing. I was at a loss for ideas, and the clock was already ticking. After much thought and consideration, I decided to take a trip to Thambuchetti in Chennai. I figured that the streets there would give me some much-needed inspiration. As soon as I reached Chennai, I started strolling around the streets. My eyes were searching for something that would spark an idea. I knew I was in luck when I saw some street vendors selling various interesting things, for it brought a ray of hope into my life. I saw them trying to attract customers with all the beautiful-looking plastic products. This gave me an idea. I realized that I could bring and sell plastic bottles and plates in my exhibition stall in Coimbatore. In those days, fascinating plastic pet bottles and plates enthralled the local Tamil populace.

Their peculiarly vivid colors and unique shapes captivated the eye, while their lightweight and novel texture delighted the touch. To the people of Tamil, these items were nothing short of a novelty.

I instantly decided to purchase the items from the local shops in Thambuchetti. I bought a variety of plastic bottles and plates of different shapes and sizes and arranged them in the Coimbatore stall with the help of my friends. They were really supportive. None of them tried to discourage me, nor did they escape from the picture when tougher tasks came up. These are the little things that I have always appreciated. There were people who left me mid-way, and I was always scared of trusting people. But then, there were people like these good friends who made me understand that not every human being is as dangerous as the ones I had seen in my past. Everything happens for a reason. People who hurt me only made me stronger in the end. Like someone once said, a rock has to be cut and polished several times to be transformed into a giant statue.

Everybody who threw stones at me, everyone who joined hands to hit me up, only gave me more energy to stand up and fight for myself. I never wanted my family to know about the things that I had to go through while I was in Coimbatore working at the bank, as I knew they would be heartbroken.

Not even once had they hit me so hard as to hurt me physically or mentally. I kept missing them every single day. I missed walking through our locality holding Mathan's hand. At this point, I knew that I badly wanted my brother to hold my hands during this event. I wanted to take him to Coimbatore and inform my friends about this decision. They were fine with it; however, they did not want to share the profit since we were not expecting a huge amount in return. Well, Mathan had already proved that he is never after money. All he was interested in was experiences and working hard to help the family somehow.

Just a month before I made up my mind to host the exhibition, I helped Mathan land a job as a sales executive. His task was to sell timeshare vacation properties. To be honest, Mathan wasn't exactly thrilled about the job. I understood his feelings because, not long ago, I had been in the same position. It was a challenging role, and I didn't want to push him into something he wasn't passionate about. But deep down, I was really excited about the idea of having him as my business partner. It felt like the perfect fit for both of us.

I asked if he would like to come and take part in this exhibition and he only said, "Why would I not? You are my big brother, and I would do anything you say." Mathan took the next bus to my locality in Coimbatore and stayed with me in my tiny little space. He never complained about the limited facilities I provided him. He was rather happy to have slept in my room and experienced everything as I did.

The next day, early in the morning, we packed the things purchased from Thambuchetti and moved to the exhibition spot. The area had already started to become crowded. We started stacking everything flawlessly on the racks and tables with great effort. We did not even have the time to look at each other's faces since we were in a hurry to sort everything out. Finally, we managed to put everything up on the tables and started waiting for potential customers.

Within the first fifteen minutes, we saw a large number of people coming close to our stall and taking a look at all our products. And then came another few customers who bought around five to six plates together, along with a couple of water bottles.

The locals ogled in wonderment as the plastic bottles and plates sparkled in the sunlight, their rainbow-like hues captivating the hearts of the local children. They excitedly ran around, pointing and chattering as they admired the beauty of the products.

Adults, too, were entranced by the beauty of the items. Many of them had never seen such a range of colors and shapes before. They appreciated the convenience of the items. What more do we even need? We felt that this was going to be a huge success. The first week passed by, showering us with an unbelievably positive response. We began to anticipate better growth in the upcoming weeks. But we do not know when a whirlwind is about to approach us and wash away all the peace of mind.

Remember what I told you earlier? You do not know when uncertainty is going to jump into the picture and play the role of the villain. Right after a week, a leading plastic utensil manufacturing company took a stall at the exhibition center, calling for a great competition.

It was a popular brand that had so many admirers that we did not even stand a chance to succeed. We were left with no option but to continue doing our work until it succeeded. I was not so emotionally affected, for I held my spirituality close to my heart. A failure is never an option.

You either succeed or learn a life lesson. I somehow was so geared up to reap the success that I went back to Chennai to pick a new product to display at the stall.

There was nothing on my mind. I was totally like a blank canvas, not knowing what to paint next. After walking through the streets for a few hours, I came across a lady selling some beautiful candle stands on the street. It looked splendid from a distance, and I was eager to know more about it. I went closer and looked at it with curiosity.

The lady looked into my eyes with the hope that I would buy something from her. She started talking to me about the price of the products, but I stopped her in the middle of the conversation. She looked at me with perplexity. To her surprise, I asked her more about the manufacturer of the product.

At this point, she knew that some good news was waiting for her. She quickly gave a detailed description of the manufacturer's place and helped me reach out to them.

I went to their remote warehouse only to remain stunned at its perfection. They made it with utmost care and passion. They had beautiful equipment with them to mold the candle stands into different spectacular shapes and sizes. I asked them if I could buy all their stock.

They were in such disbelief that they asked if I was joking. But the second I told them I was serious, I saw their expressions change from confused to delighted. Those were the moments that I had always lived for.

The beauty of life lies not in our own happiness but in the joy we bring to others. We must strive to make a positive impact on those around us and seek to bring light and love to their lives. Our lives must be marked by authentic acts of kindness and compassion rooted in a genuine desire to make a difference.

We can use our creativity to craft unique ways of connecting with others and our words to bring them comfort and solace. We must strive to live our lives with a heart full of empathy and a soul full of love for our fellow humans.

Even if the candle stands wouldn't sell well, I would still be happy about the little upward-facing curves I made on the faces of the people who made the gorgeous stands. Without a second thought, I purchased all of them. They helped me pack all the stands neatly so that it would be convenient for me to carry them on the bus.

The pack was heavy, which instantly reminded me of the times I used to travel from Munnar to Palakkad carrying the tea powder packets in huge plastic bags. In a few hours, I reached Coimbatore and unloaded the sack of candle stands at the exhibition hall. Mathan and my friends thoroughly loved the product. None of them were skeptical about the growth of the business, for they also started trusting the process rather than fogging their brains with negative thoughts. I arranged them beautifully amidst the plastic bottles and plates.

The royal candle stands became the showstopper. People rushed to take this glory home. We saw steady growth in business once the candle stands took the racks. The best part was that we were able to pitch the other products, the plates, and the bottles, so everybody who stopped to buy the candle bought the other products along with it. By the end of the exhibition, each one of us earned a profit of rupees two thousand, which was way more than my salary at the bank. I knew my intuitions would guide me on the right track and that every risk was worth taking. I realized that this is what I was born for: to become a businessman, a person who fought through all the odds of life to become a successful human being. I was all geared up to take the next big step.

My heart pounded as I took the final steps toward my destination. I knew what I had to do, and I was determined to do it with all the courage I had. I stopped in front of the head office of the bank, took a deep breath, and pushed the door open. The manager was sitting inside his cabin, staring at the huge monitor in front of him. He looked up at me, his face stern and unreadable. I swallowed hard and forced my voice to remain steady. "I have come to hand in my resignation," I said. His expression softened a little, and he nodded in understanding. I could feel my heart pounding, and I hoped I had made the right decision. I felt like I was standing on a precipice, ready to take a leap into the unknown. I gave the manager my letter of resignation, my hands shaking as I handed it over. He nodded again, and I could see the respect and admiration in his eyes. After all, I knew everything would be alright as I trusted my intuition more than anything else.

I had done the hard thing, and he knew it. They couldn't let me go that easily. The level of persuasion was pretty convincing. However, for a man who has already fixed his mind on pursuing the career of his dreams, no persuasion could be strong enough to sway him even a bit. They had to accept it and relieve me with a heavy heart the same day. I walked out of the office for one last time, feeling a strange mix of relief and pride. I made a solemn vow never to look back on the negative experiences I had endured. I promised myself to focus on the present and the future and never let the past haunt me again. I wanted to put aside my former struggles and reach higher than ever before. I wanted to find a place where I could make an impact and where I could find success and joy in my work. I knew it was possible, and I was determined to find it. I knew that I was capable of achieving my goals, and I wanted to put my energy into this instead of dwelling on the past.

After the successful completion of this exhibition, our vision became to run more shows across south India and earn profit. We decided to leave Coimbatore to host another exhibition in a different place. Mathan, who is always ready for any adventure, said a loud and clear 'yes,' but my friends were not prepared to leave the city or leave their jobs. Maybe they were not as sure about the business as Mathan and I were. Well, it is not necessary for all the passengers to stay on board till the last stop. They have to get down where they are supposed to; you can't stop them, you can't control them, and you can't even ask them for validation. I transferred their profit to their accounts, and we parted ways in the hope of meeting again next time from Coimbatore. We have to let go of people rather than forcing them to always behave according to our preferences. I have always believed that whatever you try to keep under your control forcefully will eventually leave you at the most unexpected moments. Therefore, it is always better to go with the flow.

Mathan was more than enough for me to build my empire. He has always been the strongest pillar ever. Our next exhibition was held in Pollachi. We displayed the same candle stands and attracted a number of customers who carried them home with happy hearts. We sold the candle stands for hardly thirty-five rupees. The Pollachi experiment also came out so well that we had to stop calling it an experiment further because it had already become a proper business by that time. We collected the profit, packed our things, closed the stall, and returned to Chennai to purchase more candle stands to sell at the next exhibition at Kannur in Kerala.

Traveling to a part of Kerala after so many months made me feel so good. Getting to experience the warmth of the weather gave me a different sense of pleasure. Mathan and I went to the Kannur exhibition stall to take a look at the premises, and we were truly satisfied. It was spacious and well-lit, and the best part about it was the rent.

While the rent amount at Coimbatore was twenty-eight thousand, it was just five thousand at Kannur for one whole month. This was a moment where we realized that Kerala is one of the most affordable cities in India. Visiting Kerala would never be a disappointment as the state welcomes you with immense love and warmth.

Living in Munnar in Kerala all my childhood has given me a gazillion splendid memories. With the hope of earning a fair amount of money, we opened the sacks, spread the candle stands evenly on the stands, and decorated the whole place in an attractive manner so as to attract the vibrant Keralites. But sometimes, life throws the most complicated challenges at you when you are not even prepared for them. We were expecting this to be something similar to the Coimbatore experience: successful and profitable. This time, the hurdle was the circus that was happening opposite the stall. The music was deafening, and my customers were only eager to get an entry pass to the circus and not to buy my products. My eyes were getting welled up so much that everything appeared blurred through my vision. My voice was just a barely noticeable beat in a rap song. Nobody even looked at us or our things. I was losing all my strength. My whole body started to become numb. I sat down for a while, running my hands through my hair and pressing my forehead to relieve the stress. Every time I took a pause, all that I used to think about was the purpose of my life. I started everything not to end it abruptly but to pause and reflect on my true potential and move forward so that I could raise my family and provide valuable service to the entire society. This thought has always helped me come out of every hard day that I have been through.

This time, I gathered all the spirit I could and decided to distract people watching the circus and make them come to my stall. I screamed at the top of my lungs. "This candle stand is super rare. It will keep your candles burning brighter than usual for more than eight hours," and with this, I saw several heads turning towards our stall's direction. I wiped my teary eyes and took a deeper look at their faces. Yes! They were looking at us! So many of them came up and asked for the prices and purchased the products. I looked at Mathan, and he was already staring at me. We were too surprised to see this sudden drift. I started explaining the quality of the product in an even better way, and people started talking to me. Finally, we managed to sell the complete stock within a few days. I still remember how tired we looked at the end of that exhibition. Every evening, we went to our accommodation only to squeeze liters of sweat from the shirts we wore. We always had a smile on our lips, even during the hardest of days. There were days when I held back my tears with great effort only to not make Mathan sad. Well, I still believe that he also did the same. But again, there were days when the two of us lost control, and we hugged each other and wept for long hours. These are the little moments that life throws at us. Weeping or expressing our feelings is not an indication of frailty but rather a sign of how far we have advanced, conquering all the difficulties that life has presented us. Tears are the language of the heart, and in shedding them, we communicate with the world around us and with ourselves. To be able to feel, to be able to express, is a strength that should be celebrated, for it shows that we are alive and that we are connected to our emotions. It is never a bad thing.

At the close of the exhibition, we were blessed with a bounty of fifteen thousand rupees. This gift was a reward for our hard work and dedication. We knew that all of this had been made possible by our mother. She had sacrificed her own ambitions to raise my brother and me. We decided to transfer this reward to her account as a token of our gratitude and appreciation.

We thought of all the days she had toiled and the nights she had spent worrying so that we could have a better life. We wanted to let her know that her tireless efforts had not gone unnoticed and that we were deeply thankful to her. Our home at Munnar was the only place we always went back to, as our mother was waiting for us to prepare all our favorite dishes. Every time we went back home, she embraced us with her damp and cold hands after wiping them using the end of her old aesthetic saree.

While wiping away sweat from our foreheads, she asked us a lot about everything that we had been through in the marathon to bring home fortune. She never wanted to see us struggle so much, and from our perspective, we never wanted her to suffer as well. It is what makes a family stronger- we cannot bear to see each other struggle, but we are left with zero options since life has to move on, and for that, we must dare to do the most arduous tasks. If we get stuck, it is essential to understand that life is trying to teach us a lesson.

After the success of the Kannur exhibition, we held more exhibitions in Thrissur, Salem, Coimbatore, and more.

Believe in your instincts and move forward. The world may pretend to be your cheerleader, but in reality, you are your own savior, your own defender. The world is a mere watcher of the game. You are the only player, and the ones who would unconditionally support you could only be your family.

My brother and I were driven to seek out more significant fortunes. After a brief respite in the comfort of our humble abode, we packed our bags and set out for fresh pastures in southern India. We were determined to host stalls at exhibitions and make our mark in the world.

We traversed the length and breadth of the south, admiring the vibrant culture and sprawling landscapes. All the journeys we had were filled with the sights and sounds of the bustling cities, the fragrant aroma of the country's exotic spices, and the warmth of the locals who welcomed us with open arms.

We encountered numerous opportunities, each one offering a unique experience. By this time, life had already changed in a way that we had never expected. Everything was becoming better. The days of deprivation felt like a distant memory. We had found our footing in the new decade and were determined to make the most of it.

We had to travel to more places and reap more profit. The quest for a better life is never-ending. We decided to enjoy the journey because, like Steven Furtick once said, "destination is a mirage." You may arrive at the most unexpected station. But never stop exploring opportunities.

Trust me when I say this: you have to have faith in your gut. It always leads you to the right track. If you think you should resign from your current job and start your own business, do not get stuck, not even for a moment. Go ahead and resign it right away if that could make you feel better.

Remember, you are not meant to be crushed under the thumb of poverty forever. You have all the right to live a happy life.

Takeaway-

Life doesn't always unfold as we expect. When faced with setbacks, never surrender. Fight relentlessly. If I had abandoned hope when the Kannur exhibition presented challenges, I wouldn't have made any profits. The success of the exhibition was solely due to my determination and refusal to give up. That's the magic of not giving up; the more you press on, the greater the influx of fortunes.

Mathan (Vijai's brother)

Vijai and I, despite all the hardships of our childhood, found solace in each other. We created our own little world, with its own rules and joys, and made the most out of it. Our struggles were not in vain; they only made us stronger, more resilient, and more determined to live life with grace and gratitude. Together, we crafted a life of splendor, one filled with love and laughter, and we will cherish its memory forever.

If you ask me for the best memory I had with him, I will have to tell you the story of the last forty-five years because every day spent with him was the best in its own way. One that I can remember right now is an incident that took place around 1995. After years of hard work and perseverance, we bought a pre-owned two-wheeler, a handsome Chetak. We used that vehicle to travel across south India to expand our exhibition business. One fine day, after shaking off the weariness of the day's work, Vijai proposed an interesting plan. He asked if I would go on a road trip with him from Munnar to Kodaikanal. I was thrilled like never before. When we were kids, Vijai used to take me out on our old cycle to stroll through the countryside, and I used to sit like a king in the backseat, and Vijai pedaled the cycle. After several years, when he talked about another trip, I couldn't say no.

It was a splendid day. The scooter rushed through the wet roads of Munnar with lush green tea estates and rubber plantations on either side. Tiny drops of dew hit our faces, and I saw Vijai trying to tilt his face a little towards his right and left to block the heavy drops of mist from falling onto his face, blurring his vision. Those things were not bothering me since I sat behind him. He has always been the one who protects me from every storm, and even on the bike trip, I was spared by the climate because I sat behind my big brother.

While India was under the control of the British, they had constructed several secret roads and underpasses all across the country. However, as soon as India became independent, the government took the plunge to close all those roads and convert them into forest areas. Our father had shared the story of this secret road with us and had told us that it was a hidden path leading from the misty hills of Munnar to the tranquil valleys of Kodaikanal. We were entranced by the thought of this beautiful journey and the breathtaking sights we would behold along the way. Vijai and I were absolutely fond of adventure. We were always prepared to take risks, even if it was a life versus death challenge. We made up our minds to travel through the middle of the forest without giving a second thought to the consequences. The route was only accessible to the tribes who resided in the deeper portions of the forest. They could be human eaters, or else there could be wild pigs and tigers, but little did the young blood have time to think about all this.

We kept riding in a zigzag manner, cutting through the giant trees and carefully avoiding thorns and animal traps. But the more we kept going, the more we were lost in the forest. The path started narrowing down, and our chetak started pleading with us not to twist and turn him to get through the forest. We got off the scooter and kept pulling it with us as we kept walking through the forest. After numerous hours of struggle, we managed to reach the other side, the misty Kodaikanal.

We moved to my father's elder brother's place. His son, Senthil, was older than me and Vijai, and we used to like him really very much for his kind and respectful behavior. They scolded us for taking the forest route and said that there was another road that was actually safe. But we were not ready to follow the actual route. We gathered all our courage and headed back to Munnar through the same forest road. We were confident of making it through. Unfortunately, our scooter stopped functioning unexpectedly while we were in the middle of the forest. It was not possible to go back to Kodaikanal, too, since we had already traveled several kilometers away from there. We sat on the scooter for a while, thinking about what could be done in the situation. But all of a sudden, we could hear a loud thud approaching us from a distance. We knew something was wrong and looked around to see what it was, only to realize that a herd of wild elephants was coming closer to us. What could we even do? We were stuck with no options, and we're sure that even more wild animals might come to the area. We somehow managed to survive inside the forest that night and started our journey to Munnar on foot, pushing the scooter to one side. The scooter had some technical problems, which we fixed at a local automobile shop in Munnar before heading back home. We were brave and confident all the time.

As young boys, we never had a chance to go on vacations with our families. We were too busy concentrating on work and building Royaloak step by step. The best vacation is when we finally reach home after work and spend some time with our parents. But as time passed and as our families grew bigger, we used to go on mini vacations to some resorts or hotels for around two to three days. We never felt like we needed a vacation since we all lived under one roof for over thirty-five years. After both of us moved to separate houses two years ago, there was a physical distance between us. However, it is not even deeply felt as we are still living in the same area, and we still share the food cooked at our houses every day.

Growing up with Vijai was a mix of happiness and fun and, moreover, developing the fire to grow in life. He was truly ambitious and has imparted his spirit to me as well. Our only aim, as teenagers, was to make money. Most of our relatives lived a better life right in front of our eyes, and they ignored us completely. We were not invited to any family functions and were completely treated as outcasts. Our mother worked day and night in her tiny petti shop to improve our situation. She also created a fire in us to grow and do something significant in life so that we could also have a better lifestyle. She was our role model, and she was the first entrepreneur who inspired us to become what we are. We first set some achievable goals in front of us so that we can build enthusiasm and keep our spirits high. Our first aim was to own a cycle. We were not stubborn and never wanted a new one; a second-hand cycle could have worked fine for us. We accomplished this little goal with the help of the tea powder business and bought a second-hand cycle for five hundred rupees. Before owning the cycle, we used to walk eleven kilometers to sell the tea powder in the morning and had to walk again in the evening to collect the money from those shop owners.

Our next goal was to own a scooter so that we could travel to more places to expand the tea powder business. As soon as we bought a preowned Chetak scooter, our exhibition business almost took off, and we needed an even bigger vehicle to transport and deliver the goods. We bought a Maruti Suzuki Omni van that could accommodate so many people as well as a number of things that had to be delivered.

As soon as these short-term goals were accomplished, we grew up to hit our twenties and wanted to get married and settle in life. But having our own house was mandatory to find our partners from well-off families. We dedicated the next couple of years of our lives to building a beautiful house near Kammanahalli in Bangalore. Likewise, our goals kept increasing after each milestone. When our first store was launched in Kammanahallli, we experienced a new rush of energy and confidence that eventually led us to open more stores in different parts of south India. As soon as life took a better turn following the milestones, starting from buying our first bicycle to building our own house and getting married, we chalked out our real vision or purpose in life.

Vijai has always been a great leader. He had single-handedly managed to do several things ever since he got into the field of business. I always look up to him for motivation, and I always know that he will achieve everything he manifests. The vision of Royaloak is to be a global leader, and I'm sure, under Vijai 's guidance and leadership, Royaloak would definitely make a mark in the international furniture business sector. We were South India's best furniture company before 2020, and after the entry of COVID-19, we became India's number one. I believe that Vijai will soon bring Royaloak to the top, and the world will recognize the brand in no time.

The biggest success mantra that anybody could follow is that if you love what you are doing, you will never feel like you are working, and you can completely enjoy the process. Vijai and I never got tired of working. When people normally work for eight to nine hours a day, Vijai and I work for more than sixteen hours every day. We still continue to do the same as we still don't feel like we are "working." Rather, we only feel that we are investing our time into something that we love to do with all our heart.

I have never seen Vijai in a gloomy situation, not even once in the past forty-five years. When he first started his import business, things did not go smoothly initially since we happened to receive several broken and damaged pieces. However, Vijai, being a courageous young man, decided to travel to China all by himself to check and import the best quality products to India.

A few days after Vijai returned to India, the products were transported to our warehouse in two huge containers. I had no idea about what the containers were and what they looked like. I was totally unaware of its size. Our warehouse was too congested to accommodate two huge containers of furniture. People in the locality stared at us and shouted as the containers broke several electric lines in the street; it was a Diwali day, and people were furious as electricity went off in several houses and buildings. It was Vjai's first Diwali after marriage. However, he had no other option but to stack all the goods inside the tiny warehouse with me and a few other people. We were stuck with this process until three in the morning, but the worst part of all the struggles was that we could only store fifty percent of a container inside the space we had. Several glass articles broke as we did not know how to place them properly. Vijai was never angry or disturbed by any of these events. Instead, he only said that everything would be sorted if you had the determination to do it.

We were really hardworking people; we even used to sell candle stands at exhibition stalls to earn money to make ends meet. However, selling those tiny stands for thirty-five rupees each did not help us improve our financial situation in any way. We were aware that increasing the price of the product would only lead to a huge loss. One day, as we were screaming our lungs out to attract customers, we came across a stall that was functioning opposite ours that sold TV stands. We closely observed their strategy and figured out that they took advance from their customers in the morning and delivered the stands to the customers in the evening and that they charged more than a thousand rupees for each stand. While we made three thousand five hundred every week, they were making more than that every single day. This inspired us to replicate their ideas in a better way. Vijai used to paint really well since childhood. We sat together and built TV stands with our own hands without the help of any heavy machinery or laborers but with basic tools that we had with us, and Vijai painted beautiful pictures on them. If I were to be a customer, I would surely have bought those TV stands as the pictures painted on them by Vijai were mind-blowing.

Even though our products looked great, our competitors sold better quality products, and this made Vijai think about upgrading the quality of our goods as well, after which we saw a steady increase in sales and profits. We went to the customer's houses between 9 am and 5 pm, installed the products for them, and returned with pockets full of money. People might find it hectic not to have time even to wipe their sweat, but we find our happiness in working for long hours at a stretch.

When the TV stand business took off, we began to find ways to develop this further and ended up giving rise to Royaloak. Little did we know we would become India's best furniture brand after a few years. Initially, we ourselves declared that we were the best in Bangalore, and it soon became a reality. We gradually became South India's number one and then eventually became the nation's best furniture company. It is all about manifesting positivity. Vijai taught me the importance of positive thinking and affirmations, and ever since I started following his advice, I have seen significant changes in the quality of my life.

Vijai is energetic and never sits idle, not even for a few minutes a day. We enjoy playing golf and going for long drives whenever we can. We are living life to the fullest because now, when we look back, we can see where we came from, and it is all because of our hard work and perseverance. Our uncle had once promised to take Vijai to Singapore with him for work. I was too excited as I thought Vijay would take me along with him and we could live a luxurious international life. Vijai traveled with him to Chennai to clear all the formalities and apply for a Singapore visa. But unfortunately, the uncle could not keep his promise. But today, when we look back, what I feel is that everything happens for a reason. He might have worked a regular nine-to-five job for some corporate company for a fixed salary. Now, we are in a better position because things happened the right way in one way or the other, and I'm so proud of the person my brother has become in all these years. I'm sure he will soon become a global leader.

6
THE TURNING POINT

"Life is full of surprises and serendipity. Being open to unexpected turns in the road is an important part of success. If you try to plan every step, you may miss those wonderful twists and turns."
- Condoleezza Rice

Have you ever been in a position where you had to move from one place to another without having a place to call home? Have you ever met someone and thought that God has made this person just for you? Have you seen the things you deserve naturally flowing to you in the most unexpected ways at the right time? That is the pure magic of life.

Four years flew by quicker than light, which is the speed limit of the entire planet. Thoughts about finding a life partner started ruling my mind. But how can a person like me, who is still unsettled in life, get a girl from a great background? A young boy running exhibition stalls across south India would not be a title for the world, even if it were for me. Munnar was a great place for its scenic beauty; however, the people who lived there were absolutely traditional. Certain areas of Munnar still feel like the eighteenth century, and it is a sure thing that nobody would want to send their daughters to a place like that. I was twenty-eight years old by that time. This was when Mathan and I started planning to get settled in a better city so that we could bring our parents there and find a partner from there. Initially, the first option that came to our mind was Coimbatore. After all, I had a huge history blended with tears and later happiness with the city. I got beaten up for the first time in my life in Coimbatore, but it was in that same city I had my first independent exhibition. However, I did not know whom to depend upon to find a house there. We sat confused for several days. I never had contact with any of those employees who got me the bank job. After all the criminal activities they did, I decided that I would never go back to them, even if I didn't have any friends there or even if I were to die.

One fine day, our uncle came home to pay a visit. He came to meet all of us because he had never come or talked to me after the issues that happened in Chennai. Everything rushed to my mind for a second. It's easy to cling to the past, to the pain and the anger, to the hurt and the suffering. It is easy to hold onto those things, not to let go, to stay angry and not forgive, to keep ourselves in a cycle of hurt and resentment. But there is no point in doing so. We must only move forward, build a new life, heal from our wounds, and forgive each other to have a peaceful life.

No matter what our uncle did, he surely had his own reasons, and by this time, we had already moved on from all the wounds and were ready to hold each other close once again. He was happy to see us after so long. I could finally feel relieved; I was living my life with an inner feeling that I offended him the other day, and I thought that he would never forgive me for the tone in which I shouted at him. Somewhere in between the conversation, we spoke to him about our plan to shift to Coimbatore. He had so many friends there who could help us out.

For a moment, I saw a wide smile on his face. It felt like he really wanted us to be with him. He promised to do everything he could to get us settled there, and we trusted him once again because we knew that he had a real estate business in Coimbatore back then. I was asked to provide a registration amount, which I happily gave away, hoping to have a beautiful home in a few days. And then, it was time to start waiting for the procedures to end. But the wait seemed to be never-ending.

A week passed by, and then another, and then another. We did not hear a word from him all these days in favor of us. All he told us was that the arrangements were going on and to continue to wait.

Days started becoming months, which was when we realized that, once again, he used the money that I gave him for a few other emergencies that came his way. We were devastated. We could not even ask him to return the funds since we did not know what position he was in. I still believe he had some serious issues to deal with that day.

We knew how bad it feels to have a shortage of funds when you need it the most, and therefore, we never blamed him for the situation he went through. After this event, we made up our minds to forget about settling in Coimbatore. I decided to move to Bangalore since I have heard people say that it is an amazing city where growth is constant. Also, I had never been to Bangalore and therefore wanted to explore the city.

I have heard people say its bustling streets and never-ending energy is addictive. I felt the urge to experience its vibrant feel, to witness its ever-growing skyline. I have heard tales of its glorious past, its magnificent history, and its ever-evolving present.

I knew that it was a city of technological marvels and a hub of economic progress. To me, Bangalore represents a sense of limitless opportunities, a place for growth and development. I was eager to be part of its journey and partake in its wealth of knowledge and experience. From a gazillion business opportunities to its buzzing nightlife, Bangalore is a place that sparkles with promise and energy every single day.

But before I got ready to pack my bags to enter the new place, it was necessary to have friends there. Unfortunately, I had none. But my intuition kept whispering in my ears, never to step back from this decision.

There was another exhibition that took place in Mysore, which is really close to Bangalore, which I had attended.

I used to reach the main bus stand in Bangalore at around 4 am in the morning, from where I immediately moved to Senthil's place in Balepet, but by that time, he was already in Singapore, and the house was managed by Bhoopalan, another cousin of ours. After shaking off the weariness of the long journey and splashing a handful of cold water onto my face, I took the bus to the market to purchase the goods required for the exhibition in Mysore. I returned to his flat and took the bus at midnight to Mysore and got down at the stall to arrange the products. Like every time, with lots of courage and determination, I displayed everything and kept waiting for people to come. I earned a fair profit from there and felt that the city was really warm and welcoming.

Like any other day, my few workers and I were stacking the goods on the racks to display. By that time, we had increased our list of products. We grew from plastic plates and candle stands to gas stoves and burners and several other kitchen essentials. We hosted an exchange offer where the customers could bring their old gas stoves and take away brand-new ones. We delivered the new product to the customer's house by the end of the day.

The first Mysore exhibition was, in reality, a life changer. It was held during Dussehra and to our surprise, we saw a huge crowd gathered around our stall. We almost sold out everything that day.

Once it started working out well, we brought our scooter to Mysore to hasten the delivery procedures. But there were days when we got multiple orders that went towards the Coorg area. We had been delivering stoves with our scooter for quite some time already, but we were increasingly feeling the strain. It was no longer feasible to continue this way.

We had to come up with a new solution. We began to brainstorm and pondered how we could move forward and soon realized that we needed a larger vehicle. It was time to upgrade our transport and move towards something bigger. We decided to save up money to make this happen. We finally decided on a Suzuki Omni van.

Though we were a bit hesitant to make this investment, it was the right course of action. It was a Mysore registration vehicle, and its number was 2222. People from the south of India always considered eight to be an unlucky digit. Everything that has eight in it was carefully avoided by people. The funniest thing is that people even bribe the vehicle department to get number plates without eight or a sum of eight while adding the four numbers. I was unaware of this superstition and, hence, was really happy with what I had.

The van was more spacious, allowing us to transport more items at once. It was also much more reliable and would save us time in the long run. This new van was a game-changer. We had the capacity to deliver more stoves to more locations. We were now able to expand our service and reach out to more customers. We had gone from a scooter to a van, and our business was forever changed. The only reason why we had most of our customers from Coorg was that it was really close to Mysore. Imagine getting over ten orders from the same place; you might be feeling that it would have been easy. But that's not the truth. Each delivery location, even though in the same district, was over fifty to sixty kilometers away from each other. This became a burden since petrol expenses started increasing. Gradually, kitchen gadgets proved to be a partial failure.

Again, the next day, I arranged the same things on the tables. As the crowd started rushing in, I cleared my throat, dampened it a bit with some water, and started pitching my products with all the energy I had. But this time, things were a bit different and tough. I noticed that people were least interested in my products. All the eyes were fixed on another stall that was working next to mine. They sold TV stands that were made of wood. People were moving towards them even after I screamed our lungs out, just like what happened in Kannur when the circus people were scoring better than us. We weren't kids anymore, but who said adults won't cry? I was just one step away from tears rolling down my cheeks. But giving up was not in the blood.

    I keenly observed the products the other party sold and the profit they earned from them. After observing for a couple of days, I got to understand that they sold out their complete stock before evening, took an advance amount of hundred rupees from the customer, and delivered the product to their houses in the evening after closing the stalls. That looked so innovative. The same day, I came back home and decided to recreate their business idea. While purchasing the candle stands and kitchen kinds of stuff and attracting the customers towards it consumed so much time and earned us less profit, the TV stands took less time to construct, and it was a sure thing that they could be sold for a better price which would eventually help us earn a huge profit.

NO MONEY? NO PROBLEM!

As a child, I was infatuated with painting. It was as if I was born with a paintbrush in my hand, eager to show the world my unbridled creativity. I would spend hours in my room with a blank canvas in front of me, ready to be filled with a myriad of colors. I found solace in the act of painting, an escape from the mundane reality of the world. Each stroke of a brush or dab of a palette knife brought me closer to the world of dreams, to a realm of infinite possibilities. With each painting, I felt an overwhelming sense of accomplishment. I was able to create something that was entirely my own, and I was proud of it. Like I always say, everything happens for a reason. As a kid, I used to wonder what this skill was going to win me in the future.

But once the TV stand idea popped up in our head, I started constructing them with my hands and painted beautiful pictures on them. They were like a canvas. My childhood hobby was about to become an essential skill in my entrepreneurial journey—each stroke of the brush created magic on the piece of wood. I was sure that people would love it.

The next week, we placed our brand-new product at another exhibition, and voila! We ran out of stock in no time. Ever since, Karnataka has become my favorite destination.

I realized there isn't any place like Bangalore that could help a person grow beyond expectations. It is a place of complete positivity. My spiritual mind was attracted to the energy of the city. I was eager to call it home, so I decided to stay there, hoping to build my future. I knew that I was a fortunate young man who had the willpower to achieve whatever he wanted in life. All I wanted to do was buy a property and build a house.

As soon as I landed in Bangalore, I learned about an exhibition that was about to happen at RBANMS ground, Bangalore, in 2001. This was a piece of exciting news. You might be wondering why that space is exceptionally great. It is one of the widest places in Bangalore that hosts furniture expos on a regular basis.

Getting a chance to be a part of it is like winning a tough match since it usually goes overbooked and is always extremely crowded.

But to my luck, I managed to acquire a stall there and started selling the TV stands along with the old items. In the meantime, Mathan was running another exhibition in Athur, Tamil Nadu, then. He was not that little brother anymore; he grew up to become a handsome young man who was strong enough to take responsibilities on his own shoulders. When I asked him if he could manage the exhibitions alone, all he said was that he took his inspiration from me and that he was courageous like his elder brother.

I spent some time strolling through Bangalore city to find a place to stay. Luckily, I was able to find a place, and they allowed me to stay for one month at an affordable rent amount. However, the biggest challenge I had to face there was not the climate or finding accommodation but the language spoken by the locals. Even though my grandparents were from Karnataka, I was born in Tamil Nadu and grew up in Kerala.

My language was a mix of Tamil, Malayalam, and Kannada. People often laughed at the accent. But still, I managed to sell my products well at the RBANMS ground. I started talking to people and made so many connections there. Bangalore was not fully developed like how we see it today.

There were no malls or shopping complexes. We only had a building called Safina Plaza back in 2001, which was a complex where several shops were run together. I got to know that a store was available there, and people suggested that it would be better if I shifted my things to Safina.

The thought of moving my business to a new place filled me with excitement. I knew that place was bustling with activity and was a great spot for businesses to thrive. I badly wanted to be a part of the energetic atmosphere and make a name for myself there.

With the help of Bhasker, I approached a coordinator who was in charge of the empty stall, who eventually promised to allot me a two hundred square feet area. However, what was hard to digest was that they wanted me to pay a thousand rupees every day for a week, which would cost a total of seven thousand rupees by the end of the week.

The exhibition in Kerala cost me rupees five thousand for one whole month, and therefore, this rate looked unreasonable to me. However, I was always a person who never withdrew the foot that was once placed forward. I transferred seven thousand rupees to their account and brought my goods to their store.

This time, I was totally alone. I sat down and assembled all the parts of the TV stand perfectly to make it look royal. Once everything was sorted, I went downstairs to have some food since I had been starving for the whole day, and I could hear all the rumbling noises produced inside my stomach. I had a burger from the nearby coffee shop and instantly started feeling better because an hour ago, my whole body had been completely trembling out of hunger.

I climbed the stairs up again to stand at the stall and wait for customers. The first day passed by with zero sales. This was indeed heartbreaking. I came back to my room with a heavy heart and sat down on my bed for a while to process the feeling in my head. The night felt too long. I stared at the ceiling, thinking about what to do. But I was not worried about tomorrow. What if a miracle happens, and everything gets sold out really quickly? Well, it can happen the other way around, too. We do not know what life is going to throw at us. I was ready to wait for the surprise, be it favorable or not. All this while, my cousin Bhaskar turned out to be a staunch supporter. He was a research scientist at the National Research Centre, and he had been in Bangalore for the past few years. He was no different from Senthil. We were all more like best friends. I was never expecting him to show up and help me at the exhibition place by leaving his actual well-paid job behind for a few days. He educated me about the life and lifestyle of Bangalore. He took me to several places to explore the unending beauty of the city. He gave me the best advice of my life regarding the art of business. He stood at the shop with me without hesitation. He kept me motivated so much that I really forgot how bad I felt when nobody came to the store the first day.

Sometimes, everything we were hoping for might never happen. It all depends upon luck. The second day came with a new ray of hope. I woke up to the narrow stream of sunlight entering my room through the open window; I felt energized and jumped out of bed to start the day. Like the previous day, I went to the store in Safina Plaza and stood there for hours waiting for customers to come in.

Unlike normal exhibition stalls, you cannot really shout out and pitch the products to attract customers to your shop when you work inside a mall or a shopping complex, and for this reason, I had to maintain decorum. Unfortunately, the second day also ended, and I did not earn even a single rupee. And then came the third day. I did not give up on hope. But that day almost affected a quality I have always had- my confidence.

Nobody came in or enquired about the TV stands, and I started feeling like I had lost all the money and time. Is this even my place? Am I even supposed to be here? Will I be successful any time soon? This was a sign of decline.

We did not have enough money to afford the rent for another week. I called the truck driver who helped me transport my goods from RBANMS to Safina Plaza and asked him to come on Sunday and take everything back to RBANMS ground.

Four days passed by without even a single sale, and that almost gave me trauma, but on the fourth day, which was a Friday, Bhasker, my cousin, joined me at the shop. He showered me with immense moral support and the same day, I was able to sell two TV stands.

I was hoping Saturday to be a good one as I had Bhasker next to me. The first half passed by with just one sale. However, before closing the shop for the day, we were able to sell three more stands, making it a total of four that day. This showed a sign of improvement. It was two the previous day, and therefore, four was definitely a good number. We wanted to keep the shop open on Sunday as well, but the building coordinator was reluctant to let that happen. After a prolonged conversation with her, we managed to convince her and kept the store open. Luckily, we could sell seven TV stands and that day and that was the best Sunday ever.

By 8.30 in the night, I called the truck driver and asked him not to come and informed him that I was planning to extend the business for one more week at Safina Plaza. However, I was faced with a dilemma. I had asked the coordinator lady for permission to use the shop for an extra week, but she had not responded. I knew that if I didn't get the chance to show off my products, all my hard work would be for nothing. I mustered up my courage and approached her again. I could sense her reluctance, and my heart sank, but I pushed on. I explained why I needed the extra week and how it would be beneficial for both of us. I begged her to consider my request. She was silent for a few moments and then nodded her head in agreement. I was elated! I thanked her profusely and began making preparations for the upcoming week. The extra week of preparation was invaluable. I was able to create a beautiful display and carefully arrange my products. I hoped that the customers would be impressed and that I would be able to make some good sales. Soon, we started selling more than two stands every day, which earned us great profit. That was enough for us to afford the rent and food for quite some time.

But deep inside, we knew that we wanted something beyond this. We wanted our own shop where we could stay for as long as we wanted and not a place from where we could get kicked out at any moment. Finding a life partner was also equally important. Sales were going pretty well at Safina Plaza, and all around me, I heard the cheerful hum of customers and vendors.

Suddenly, my phone rang, and my mother was on the other end. "I have a proposal for you," she said. "A woman from Coimbatore, a city very close to yours, is looking for a groom. She is a beautiful and intelligent woman, and she comes from a good family. Would you like to know more about her?" The idea of having a woman from Coimbatore as my companion sent a wave of excitement through me. I thought of the possibilities that could come from such a union. I imagined us traveling together, exploring new places, and learning about each other. I thanked my mother for letting me know about it, and told her that I would love to consider it. As I hung up, I felt a surge of optimism. All my life, I had never wanted to fall in love with someone as I believed that falling in love would deviate me from my aim. To me, love was a distraction rather than a feeling. I wanted a well-arranged marriage, and this proposal from Coimbatore was something that I was really looking forward to making happen. In the past, there were times when people were not allowed to meet each other before marriage, and for that reason, I could not go and meet the girl. Her father, who was an IFS officer, came to Bangalore to take a look and see if I possessed the qualities that he was expecting his son-in-law to have. On visiting my temporary stay, where the roof was covered with an asbestos sheet where the rent was just two thousand four hundred rupees, he was extremely disturbed and disappointed that he rejected the proposal. I had never seen his daughter before, but I was hoping that this would work out, and for a moment, I felt shattered. But I thought to myself that I would prove my worth one day.

Once I started earning a steady income, I decided to build a new house near Kammanahalli. The feeling of finally getting a chance to have our own "home" was something that was unimaginable for me until two years before. Bangalore turned out to be my home, and I knew that for sure; my intuitions kept whispering that in my ears.

Now I finally have a place to build my roots, a place for my family to call "ours."

I was planning to buy 30 to 40 square feet of land, but my cousin Bhasker made me realize that I deserved better than that, and he asked me to buy 40 to sixty square feet of the area. He taught me how to bargain with cement dealers and other people who charged unreasonable prices for materials. I assigned the construction works to a contractor named Zubair, who thereafter helped me a lot in constructing my dream home. While the construction works were going on in full swing, I happened to receive another proposal, that too, once again, from Coimbatore. They were also from the business sector.

They owned a textile shop in Tamil Nadu named "Rukmini Textiles" that sold expensive silk sarees. The couple had two daughters who were studying at Nirmala College in Coimbatore. They drove themselves to the college in their own car, which clearly indicated that they belonged to a wealthy family. Their father came and visited the place where I lived, and once again, I got rejected for the temporary job and the shabby rented house.

At that moment, I understood that the ultimate goal for most parents was to secure a stable future for their daughters, a future that was prosperous, one that was free of financial worries and burdens. Mathan and I decided to open a new furniture store in Bangalore so that we could have an independent space for ourselves. We never said no to experiments and experiences. With the little profit from Safina Plaza and all the savings we had, we decided to take an eight hundred square feet shop near Kammanahalli main road for rent. But luckily, one of our suppliers said that his uncle owned that store, and he wanted me to buy it. That became our first-ever independent store. All our relatives and friends were invited to the inauguration ceremony of the new store.

Apart from Bhasker, two of our other cousins, Bhoopalan and Suresh, also helped me a lot during this journey. They even took me to a place in Vijayanagar to check out a house that I could buy. Even though I skipped the deal, they never got offended. They kept helping me even more. Every morning, we met at Avenue Road for breakfast and used to go house hunting before I bought the land. All this time, our major source of income was still Safina Plaza. However, in 2006, a big and popular brand decided to open their store in Madiwala, Bangalore. The owner of the brand approached me once and requested that I display a few of my products in their shops. Even though the profit was not that commendable, I still accepted his request, and therefore, I had two sources of income. From the moment I opened the doors to my own store in Kammanahalli, I was determined to make it a success. I worked tirelessly to ensure that it was a pleasant place to shop, with friendly staff and a wide selection of products. I always kept a keen eye on the quality, making sure that my selection stayed up to date. I was always striving to make the store better. I would regularly re-organize the shelves and displays to make the store more inviting and easier to navigate. I also worked to bring in new stock and develop relationships with suppliers to ensure that the store had the latest items in stock. Gradually, I began to display sofa sets and dining sets at the store.

Life had begun to settle, and I had almost reached a comfortable place. I was content with my life and had made peace with the decisions I had made. But then, one day, my brother Mathan came and shook up my world. "Why can't we approach that girl whose proposal you received last year?" He asked me, his eyes wide with curiosity.

This kept me awake for a few days and nights. "Well," I said, "now that the construction of our house is in the final stage and we are officially entrepreneurs, I could give it one more try, right?" I approached my mother and asked her to connect me with the second beautiful young lady from Coimbatore whose proposal she had brought a year ago.

After a few days, her father once again visited my place, only to be stunned to see the progress that had been made within a year's time. He was more than impressed that he finally decided to introduce his daughter to me. I will never forget the place where we first met. Even though I was not that religious, our first meeting happened at a place on top of the Palani temple.

There she was, Maheshwari, a graceful young woman who looked like a goddess with her long, thick black hair lying straight, her skin that glowed brighter than the afternoon sun, and her smile that was addictive.

I couldn't think about anything else. We have been so into each other since the first day we met. We visited each other's house and finally tied the knot on the 10th of March, 2004.

That is life. You may get rejected several times. But each rejection is a sign of a better tomorrow. There is nothing like "the end" to something. Everything that looks like an ending could be the beginning of a significant event.

Together, Maheshwari and I started building a future. We shared ideas and stayed close to each other through everything that came into our lives thereafter. Our marriage was one of the biggest turning points of my life.

She was my soulmate; if not, why did she not get married to somebody else after her father first rejected me? What is meant for us will always find its way to us, or else Maheshwari wouldn't have been mine today.

It was written in the stars, or maybe it was a result of what I wished on a shooting star when her father first rejected me. In the end, the only truth is that what is meant to be, will be, and what must be yours will be yours, no matter what comes in the way.

Takeaway:

Good things always take time. You need to be extremely patient, but that doesn't mean you need to stop putting effort and just wait. Keep working hard and one day everything will happen in your favor. Have faith in your intuitions.

Listen to your gut; it never lies.

Mrs. Maheshwari Vijai (Vijai's wife)

Vijai has always been a brave young man. When COVID hit in 2020, and the whole world became a sinking ship, Royaloak not only managed to survive but flourished splendidly due to Vijai's confidence and courage. He changed everything from offline to online.

The entire COVID-19 time, I would say, was a significant turning point for the whole family. We were all together in one place. My sister and brother-in-law also moved in with us to our new house exactly one day before the lockdown. We moved into a villa. That was the best thing we did, or else we would have been isolated in different places and would have been in a bad state of mind. For two months, they were with us. It was a big turning point as a family, and we had lots of conversations. We kept discussing how we were going to take Royaloak forward. We noted down the next steps, and I think a lot of teamwork happened during that period. My sister, my brother-in-law, Vijai, and I worked really hard together during those days, and it was really rewarding in the end. Actually, I would say it was so positive. I don't know how many companies really worked during COVID. But Royaloak really worked out well during the tough times. Our official meeting started at nine in the morning, and there were back-to-back meetings. We were able to survive; I wonder how many companies earned enough profit to pay the salaries of their employees, and it is a matter of fact that several companies had to shut down after being unable to recover their losses. But Royaloak did it- we did what was impossible for others. We only had fifty stores before the lockdown, and after the lockdown, we were able to sign agreements for over seventy more stores across south India.

I think the major support Vijai had was from his brother, Mathan. They are very strong, and that is a result of the way they grew up. Our kids, right now, are being raised in a more sophisticated way. Everything is spoon-fed to them. But for Vijai and his brother, their parents had to suffer every single day to bring home a day's meal because food is the main criterion. Vijai had gone through a lot more than we could even imagine earning a living, and the best part is he did everything in the best possible way. They're very strong. I think these people are really brave, and that's what I have been seeing them doing for all these years. It's been nineteen years since I got married to Vijai, and ever since, I have seen him as a very strong and very brave individual. Both Vijai and Mathan make the best decisions every single day, and they never become tired of facing obstacles. What they believe is that the bigger the problem, the more the mind will function powerfully- they never ignore problems. Every human being will have tensions and mixed emotions during tough situations, but what I have seen to date is that Vijai was never tense about anything. He has the caliber to handle everything in the best possible way.

He does not postpone things; I have never heard him say things like, "No, let's do it later." He does all the tasks on his checklist the very day itself. He tried to sort things out as quickly as he could. I understood the height of their confidence, bravery, and decision-making skills when they decided to open stores during COVID-19. We didn't know what was going to happen the next moment, but still, they took the initiative to take risks. Vijai has changed so much in these nineteen years of marriage. When we first met, Vijai was 29, and I was 23. What maturity can we expect from a young 29-year-old man? However, Vijai proved he was the most talented individual by starting his entrepreneurial journey at a very young age. In these 19 years of our blissful married life, I have witnessed him molding himself into a better person every day. I would say he is a self-made entrepreneur. He wants to do his things, even the minutest ones, in a really nice way, and he gets involved in everything effortlessly. His interest in things like painting and drawing is also a result of his own commitment to a passion, and his body taught him how to do it. He puts one hundred percent of his commitment into everything he does. Working with Vijay is the best thing that has happened in my life in the past few years. He guides me in so many ways when sometimes I'm stuck somewhere, and definitely, he's always been there for me, not just to pick me up when I fall but to prevent me from falling. It's easy for me to work with him under his guidance. If you ask me what kind of relationship I would love to share with Vijai, I would, any time, pick our husband-wife relationship over everything else. He inspires me every minute of the day with his workaholic and lovable personality. A lot of houses have different routines, you know, maybe sometimes, on Monday, you feel lazy and might not want to wake up, or you may not want to work, but this man, I don't know how, but every day follows the same routine. Not even on holidays does he change his routines. Although I try to follow his schedule, I fail most of the time; I do try to catch up. Maybe on some days, he's up by 3.30 am, and I'm maybe up by five or half past five. But on such days, I try to push my kids to follow their father so that they will also have a disciplined life. Vijai is a man who has proved that a healthy daily routine and discipline make you a completely happy person throughout the day. If there is no discipline, you can't find happiness in the little things you achieve. Vijai motivates not only me but also the workforce at Royaloak by demonstrating how to execute discipline and how to communicate in a pleasant way.

He is a spiritual person who wakes up early in the morning for meditation, which is helping him drive the business forward in a healthy way, making Royaloak stand out from the crowd.

When Vijai's proposal came to me for the first time, my father was not ready to give his daughter to him, but when he approached for the second time, my father agreed to get me married to him. It's not my faith but my father's faith, I would say, that led to our marriage. My father believed this man was going to do something really good in life. When Vijai first came up with the marriage proposal, they were settling in life. They had one small store in Safina Plaza, and they were doing exhibitions. But on the split side, I come from a completely settled background. So, when this proposal came up, my father, just like any other father, was definitely hesitant to send me there. But then Vijai waited for a year, worked really hard, and then approached my family once again. But this time, he was in a far better position, and my father nodded a yes to our union. I have always believed that my father chooses the best for me, and when my father started believing in Vijai, I, too, invested my trust and love in him. But it is awesome right now. I'm married to this handsome young man, and I am very proud of him. There are so many things he is achieving, and I feel more than happy for him.

I am really happy that Vijai is finally writing a book. This makes me feel very special. He is an amazing person who does everything in a positive way. When things get tough in business, we support each other, and we try to talk more about the problems and try to sort them out rather than ignore them. When something ever goes wrong, the best thing we do is support each other mentally and emotionally.

Vjiai has faced a lot of ups and downs throughout his life, and his China trip was one of the most terrible downs he went through. About three months after our wedding, he said he was going to China. I did not know how to respond because I was not mature enough to understand the seriousness of it. We dropped him at the airport and came back. But even after several hours, we did not receive any calls or letters from Vijai, and that was the moment when I faced an extreme panic situation. However, I managed to accept the fact that Vijai might have lost access to his Indian SIM card. Thankfully, he called me as soon as he bought a Chinese sim card, and I felt relief after that. I started waiting for him to come back so that I could get some time to spend with him. Within a few more days, he called from China to inform me that he was flying back, and I was on cloud nine from that moment. As soon as he reached back home, Vijai started narrating the whole episode of things he had to go through, and all I did was listen to it like some interesting story. But, after several years since this incident took place, I realized the seriousness of the situation. I realized how difficult it is for a man to travel to an unknown country with nobody to support him from behind. Now, at this point, too, I keep telling myself how brave my husband is. He could have stopped himself from traveling to China, considering the fact that he does not know how to communicate in the Chinese language. But he still took that step, and that is what makes Vijai special. Even today, he never refuses to face tough times in life. He always says that it is fine, let us do it. He never says the word NO to the kids as well. If the kids want to jump, Vijai lets them jump; if they want to run, he lets them run rather than asking them not to for fear of them falling or getting hurt. Our eldest daughter is eighteen, the second one is thirteen, and the youngest one is nine. Although the three of them are very close to me, they make all the important decisions in their lives only after discussing them with their father. Our kids consider their father as their hero. When we grew up seeing heroes in movies, my kids were fortunate enough to grow up with a real-life hero.

They sometimes type Vijai's name on Google and read through articles featuring Vijai, and sometimes read the reviews on the Royaloaks' official site. They even talk about their plans to take over the company someday in the future. The eldest son says he will take the major portion of the company. It is fun to see how a thirteen-year-old and nine-year-old plan and discuss taking charge of an organization and all the responsibilities that will follow. Vijai, at my kid's age, had to work hard to afford a day's meal. They had the rawest form of childhood.

They were, of course, naughty and were always out doing wild things. I can't even think of letting my kids do such things in the world we live in today. Vijai's parents gave both of them the freedom to do anything they wanted to, and that is the secret of their success. Vijai and Mathan once went on a trip to Kodaikanal from Munnar on their Chetak scooter, but unfortunately, the scooter stopped moving after they entered a forest that looked haunting. I can't imagine letting my children go on a bike trip through the middle of the forests.

What if some animals try to attack them? These boys were not bothered about any such things. They stayed in the middle of the forest for one night until they could clearly see the roads the next morning and pushed the scooter to the other end of the forest with great effort. Who would even dare to do things like that these days?

When they first bought a car, neither Vijai nor Mathan knew how to drive a car, and nobody in the family could have taught them how to drive. But they did not wait for someone to help them. They learned the skill all by themselves. I'm proud to say that my kids are following in their father's footsteps. They also love to learn new things by themselves. They are also so much into adventure and such interesting activities. Sometimes, I used to get tense on seeing them doing certain things, but Vijai asked me not to worry and encouraged our children so much. Vijai and the kids play golf on weekends, and I love to watch them play. It is indeed a rare kind of happiness to see nineteen years of pure marital bliss with three lovely kids. It is even more beautiful to see my children growing up to look like my husband one day. I'm so proud of Vijai. Dear Vijai, keep going, and you will reach your goals one day for sure.

NO MONEY? NO PROBLEM!

Bhaskar (Vijai's cousin)

Although Vijai and I have been cousins, we never met during childhood. The first time we met was when Vijai came to my house in Bangalore in 2001. I guess it was somewhere in the middle of June. Back in our hometown, Vijai's house and mine were separated by a common wall. But they never lived there as Vijai's parents kept moving to different places in Kerala and Tamil Nadu. I saw him as a child just once, and then he ran and played around with his brother outside the house. So, our first official meeting happened in 2001. By that time, Vijai was running a stall in Bangalore to display some products. He managed to find out my number and address, and that made me feel so good. His first stall in RBANMS ground went well for around forty days and was about to be over. He wanted to find a way to manage to settle in Bangalore. He wanted me to help him figure out a way. After doing my research, I found out that Safina Plaza would be an excellent place for Vijai to start his business. Back then, there weren't any malls like the ones we have today in Bangalore. The only building complex where people came to shop was Safina Plaza, and I thought it would be an ideal place for Vijai to set up his products. I stood with him as a strong supporter and helped him get into Safina Plaza. It wasn't easy to acquire space in the building, but we managed to make it through together.

He is really calm, and he never gets offended by people's comments. I felt so good to know that he has immense patience within him. He asked me about how to do certain things, and I imparted all the knowledge I had to him so that he could do something significant in his life.

He is a very positive person. One fantastic quality I noticed in Vijai is that he never responds to people in the impulse of a moment. When we ask him a question, he takes a couple of seconds to contemplate and responds to the question once he has a proper answer to it. I have not found such positivity in anybody else before.

While Vijai was busy building his empire in Bangalore, Mathan was engaged in another exhibition in another location in south India.

They supported each other really very much. Once Mathan was done with the exhibition, he moved to Bangalore to support Vijai at Safina Plaza. After coming to Bangalore, Vijai decided to settle there, and for that reason, he never left the city. There was a time when he faced a stage of loss at the business he was doing in Safina Plaza. He asked me about what could be done; he wanted to leave that building and move to a different location to continue crafting his dream. There were a number of materials that he had to take back from Safina Plaza. However, he managed to shift the business to another location and sell out all the TV stands he had with him within a short period of time.

Vijai used to come to my place for lunch and dinner, and we used to sit and talk for long hours. Slowly, he achieved so much in life. They had purchased a second-hand Omni van by the time. However, Vijai told me that Mathan and he were planning to buy another van.

I was so thrilled that I accompanied Vijai to a car dealer, and we selected a good-condition Maruti Omni van together. The number of it was 2222, and I feel delighted to see that he still uses the same number for all the vehicles that he owns. I have been with him through almost all of his life-changing moments.

I worked for the central government as a scientist, so I didn't have to work on Saturdays and Sundays. That time was an opportunity for me to go to Safina Plaza with Vijai to help him out in everything I could.

There were several weeks when I sat with him at the stall from Wednesday to Sunday to make him feel confident. On some days, I used to go directly to the shop from the office so that I could support him and help him sell more goods. He had to go through several ups and downs like any other businessman, but in the end, he managed to succeed.

I had never imagined that his growth would be so exponential. All I knew was that he would have an image and identity for himself and that he would grow steadily in the firm. But instead of just being a known brand in the little circle of Karnataka, Royaloak grew exponentially to become the number one furniture brand in India.

I firmly believe that the secret to Vijai's success is the hardships and struggles he had to go through in his adolescence age and the courage he showed to come out of it through hard work. They saw all sorts of tough times before the age of twenty. They had to work really hard for everything, from food to education. They grew up knowing the worth of every single penny they spent and earned. They were sincere and put their complete efforts into whatever they did. Both Vijai and Mathan are so attached to their family that they never stay away from each other. It is incredible to see how they have a beautiful work-life balance. They deserve more than what they already have, considering everything they have been put through due to circumstances, and I'm sure they will conquer more heights and will emerge as even more successful people in the future.

7

ACCOMPLISHING PROFESSIONAL GOALS AT AN EARLY AGE: A TRIP TO CHINA

"Keep my word positive. Words become my behaviors. Keep my behaviors positive. Behaviors become my habits. Keep my habits positive. Habits become my values. Keep my values positive. Values become my destiny."
— Mahatma Gandhi.

Have you been through a situation where you had to bear the brunt of someone else's mistake? Do you think you must always sit and wait until someone comes to rescue you from your desperate state? Would you show the courage to stand up for yourself and do your things on your own without waiting for a mediator to help you out?

Launching a business with a skeptical mindset would lead the company to a state of damage before it even takes off. Having an absolutely positive outlook is essential to the best of any startup. I used to be a person who takes life as it comes; it was all la vie en rose for me, for I never viewed anything through the lens of negativity. When life throws stones at you, pick them up, polish them, and show the world how you can build a mansion out of them. I went through the thickest of challenges when I opened my first independent furniture store in Kammanahalli. We named it Oak and Oak as we knew that oak is one of the most robust trees in our country and has thick trunks and wide branches. We wanted our company to spread across the country like an oak tree and provide shade and comfort to everyone who walked through the city. We wanted people to remember us as the brand that offers the best furniture. Ever since childhood, I knew that my fortune lay in business as I was able to go through every sort of hardship with ease. However, when Oak and Oak was launched, all I had with me to display in my new store was a few TV stands that I had made all by myself. Although they looked breathtakingly stunning, it was essential to have some other great collection in place to attract potential customers. What more than a TV stand could I even make? I asked myself. The thoughts that rushed to my mind were like stars in the night sky, each one bursting with possibility.

Within a few moments of introspection, I found the perfect solution to my dilemma, lighting up my mind like the sun in the morning sky. I looked around me and took a stroll through the streets of Bangalore, following the positivity my mind had spread in front of me. After a few hours, I came across a shop that resembled an international shopping place, wide, colorful, and bright. The shop was occupied by several colorful wooden articles and furniture. The shop was already visible from a distance, and I was tempted to go closer and take a look at the beauty. Conversations with the shopkeeper enlightened me with an outstanding idea. All of his products were imported from China, and he was clearly making a massive profit out of it. I badly wanted to give it a try and see how well it worked.

As soon as I got to know about this, I knew it was time to take the plunge and start my own import business. I had always been fascinated by the intricate designs and craftsmanship of Chinese furniture, and I was sure that the market would be there to support my enterprise. I began researching the furniture importation business and found out that there was a lot more to it than I had known till then. I had to learn how to select and transport the furniture and how to price it competitively. I learned I would also be responsible for marketing and staying up to date with the latest and most attractive trends in the industry. I was fortunate to find a reliable importer from Chennai who could provide me with the furniture I needed. Everything started moving forward really quickly, and within no time, I started receiving my packages.

With all the excitement of having begun a new chapter of life, I began to open the boxes one by one, only to be broken deeply. Most of the furniture that I bought with all my little savings came in damaged; some were like puzzles that lost several pieces, some were broken and needed to be fixed, and there were some that couldn't be restored no matter how hard we tried. Nobody was pleased with this incident, and they all pointed their fingers at my import business plan. People blamed me so much. Although the products in the cargo were mostly damaged, I was undeterred. I saw this as a challenge, and I was determined to rise to it with a positive attitude.

I began by carefully assessing the condition of the goods and sorting them into categories to figure out what could be salvaged. Those items that were broken beyond repair were set aside, and the rest were taken to my workshop. I set to work, repairing and refurbishing the items. Where necessary, I replaced broken parts and reassembled them. I sanded down surfaces that were scuffed or scratched and repainted them with fresh coats of paint. I worked diligently and with great attention to detail, ensuring that the products were of a high standard before I put them up for sale.

I allowed myself to hope, to dare to dream of the possibilities. With patience and faith, I waited for the good news that I knew was on its way. And when it came, it was more beautiful than I ever imagined. My efforts paid off, and customers began to take notice of my stock. They were well attracted to the glittery products and items made of glass. Soon, I had a steady stream of customers, all pleased with the quality of my goods. The products were affordable for everyone.

Once, when my family never had a chair to sit on, I used to walk past many furniture stores in the town, thinking how lucky those people who could afford those beautifully crafted designer chairs would be. It only looked like a far-stretched dream to me back then. We never served dinner on tables. The broken floor was the only table we could afford. Instead of steel spoons, we used coconut shells tied tightly to bamboo sticks to make them look like a spoon, and sometimes, we even made them using the raw leaves plucked from the branches of jackfruit trees. Growing up, we were only happy and never complained about the past. All we thought about was making the future a better one, not just for us but for everyone. This became our primary purpose when Royaloak was launched. Our products became a part of even the most miniature houses in the town. It was made for the rich and poor alike without any discrimination.

However, by the time the business started to flourish, receiving damaged products had become a regular event. We never received a cargo that contained everything we ordered. The worst part was that we did not even receive the goods on a regular basis. Every time I raised a question about this, the delivery person kept saying that he would make sure those missing parts were delivered with the next cargo. That was his trick to escape from being scolded by my friends, who were also into the furniture import business back then. They did everything they could have done to make me step back from depending on these people and stop wasting money on damaged goods. Who would even be happy to see people spending money on useless things? There were times when we received wardrobes without doors and bedside tables without drawers and had to spend days to re-create them using our equipment and hard work. When this became intolerable, I contacted the agent in Chennai who was in charge of importing goods. He helped me for a while, but things even got out of his hands, too. As time passed, these issues kept recurring, and we kept losing our precious time. This had to be fixed. I sat down, contemplating the problem that lay before me. I appointed another agent in Chennai to send me the Chinese imported goods directly when they reached their main hub due to customer demand. But I was not really satisfied. I somehow had to come up with a solution, a way to make everything right again. As the hours passed, my thoughts drifted in and out, each one bringing in a set of uncertainty. After days of meditation and proper thinking, I witnessed a ray of hope approaching me from the least expected direction. It was a difficult road ahead, but I was confident that I could make it work. I set out to make my plan a reality, confident that I could make a difference. I decided to travel to China and import the furniture by myself rather than depending on anyone else.

When hard work and luck come together, everything turns magical, and it knocks in like a surprise. While I sat desperate, not knowing how to find an alternate option to resolve my issue, I received a call from Mr. Gopal Ram from Chennai, whom we can consider the first person in India to introduce the idea of importing Chinese furniture to our country. He promised to introduce one of his most trusted manufacturers from China to me and said he would pick me up from Hong Kong as soon as I reached there. This way, he promised that my import business would be a huge success. I was more than thrilled about it. But then, a trauma from the past started to haunt me like a nightmare. What if I could not go to China? Will it come to an abrupt failure like the Singapore event? It had been ages since I was over that incident, but, as a matter of fact, a human mind is a machine that never forgets anything forever. But I never allowed the negativity to rule my mind.

I was aware that I was supposed to have a visa to travel to a different country. But as per Gopal's instruction, I had to reach Hong Kong first and then apply for my visa on arrival. Within a few days, I moved my pawns in the direction of success and decided to travel to China to take care of everything all by myself; I was not ready to give up and pick up some other career options since becoming an entrepreneur has been my oldest wish and to fulfill this dream, I booked my tickets real quick.

This was the biggest adventure trip of my entire life as an adult. I packed and carried a tiny little suitcase with only a few essential things and headed to the airport with my mother, brother, and my darling wife to whom I was married just three months ago; I really wished I could take Maheshwari along with me, but it was not possible in the last moment. I waited for over a year to bring her into my life, and we wished to travel together from the day we got married. But this trip could neither be canceled nor could I have taken her along. I kissed her on the forehead and promised to come back soon. Tiny pearls rolled down her dark brown eyes. I wiped it once, and for the second time, I did not even turn around to look at her; I was busy rubbing my eyes to control my emotions to look brave in front of her. I pushed the luggage trolley towards the ramp to enter the airport counter to get my boarding pass. It was my first time inside an airport, and I was confused about so many things.

After receiving the boarding pass, I looked out of the glass window close to the entrance only to see my family waving their hands at me and blessing and wishing me good luck. With the energy and positivity that came to me from them at that moment, I headed towards the main gate.

While falling slightly asleep on the silver airport chair, I was woken up by an announcement that informed all the passengers to move toward their respective gates. I walked through the tunnel connecting the airport and the flight and located my seat with the help of the air hostess. The flight took off with a little jolt. I was getting closer to my destination; I could hear my heartbeat outside. The plane rushed through the clouds against the wind, and the wings were jerking due to the force of the current.

The next day, the flight landed at Hong Kong airport. Standing inside an international airport gave me goosebumps. But I was clueless about what was going to happen later on. As soon as I stepped into the airport, the first thing I tried to do was to get in touch with my agent. This was when I realized my SIM card wouldn't work anymore. I did not know how to ask for help. The most horrifying part of being in a country like China is that people deliberately chose not to communicate in English. Everyone in Hong Kong stared at me as if I was an alien. None of them responded to the queries I made in English. However, I couldn't run away from the situation and had to find a way out to call my agent. After a lot of confusion and tension, I managed to convert Indian currency to Hong Kong dollars and dialed up my agent using a calling booth inside the airport. My voice was shaking when I asked him why he wasn't there at the airport. The tension and stress in my tone were none of his concerns that he, not even in a consoling manner, said he would wait for me at the Shenzhen border. But even then, I didn't have a Chinese visa. He asked me to approach counter number six to get it done. After a bunch of broken communication and headaches, I reached out to counter six and applied for my visa. They asked me to wait for eight hours. I slept in the chair opposite the counter for a while, not knowing where to go. My head started falling sideways, but I shook the weariness and sat erect. But my eyes were shutting down really hard that I could not even control them after a point. After six hours of broken sleep, I was summoned to the sixth counter to receive my passport with my visa printed on it. Now, that was a little bit relieving.

After stepping out of the airport, I took bus number twelve to a place that was almost in the middle of Hong Kong, as instructed by the agent. From there, I had to take a train to Shenzhen, where I was supposed to clear the immigration formalities and acquire permission to cross the Shenzhen border. The agent promised to pick me up from the station. Like a child waiting for his mother at the kindergarten, I kept waiting for the manufacturer's agent to arrive, but he never turned up, and I was left in despair. Instead, he asked me to take the train to Shenzhen and said he would be there. And here comes the next challenge- buying tickets from the station.

Although I was shaking from head to toe, I took a deep breath and waited in the queue for my turn. As each one of them moved out of the line with tickets in their hand, my heart started beating faster as my turn was almost around the corner. The person who was standing in front of me was buying his tickets to someplace that I had not even heard of before, and I attempted to overhear what he was saying. However, I could not even understand a single word as they were speaking the Chinese language.

When it was finally my turn, I pleaded with him to speak in English and told him that I was lost. The person at the counter was kind enough to understand the situation that I was in, and he communicated adequately and handed over my ticket to Shenzhen. I believe I created traffic there that day. It felt like when some people formed a crowd at the Indian railway ticket counter, counting currency and enquiring about unnecessary things. The air was charged with excitement as I stepped up to the counter to purchase my first train ticket from China. I couldn't believe it was really happening; the thought of my journey stirred up a wave of emotions. With a sense of elation and a smile on my face, I handed over my money and stepped away with my ticket in hand. The feeling of pride and satisfaction I felt was overwhelming. I had the ticket, and I was on the path to discovering something new. I was invigorated and ready for the adventure that lay ahead. I walked away from the queue with a newfound confidence and a heart filled with joy and anticipation.

But still, I was worried about whether the agent would show up at least at the Shenzhen border to help me with the immigration or not. I had to contact him but could not find a calling booth anywhere around. Thankfully, I was able to purchase a Chinese SIM card from a nearby place. However, after the call, I learned that he wouldn't be coming to pick me up after the immigration procedures. Rather, he sent a friend of his, who took me to a tiny hotel room. Even though it was clean and tidy, it did not have enough facilities and was not comfortable.

I was wondering if I would end up living inside that box for the rest of the days. The wall looked pure white with soothing warm lights and led on the borders. The bed was covered in a huge white quilt that felt like a piece of cloud. The walls had unique Chinese pictures embossed on them. The fragrance of the interior was so good that I wished I could carry that home. The only problem was its size: tiny and congested. However, I was only concerned about the next few days. I wanted to fulfill my purpose. The next day, I was taken to Foshan City on a bus that looked luxurious compared to the buses in India. A journey on one of those buses was truly a magical experience.

The Chinese air was mostly filled with the sound of the engine, the passengers talking, and the occasional honk of a car. But to me, nothing could ever beat the beauty of Indian culture. As soon as the bus reached its destination, I walked out of the bus to take a look at the wide interlocked footpaths and neatly tarred roads. What a city!

The streets of Chinese cities were alive with beauty; the hustle and bustle of the people and the vibrant colors of the buildings created a unique and captivating atmosphere. In the morning, the sun's rays peeked through the tall buildings, casting its warm light across the streets. At night, the bustling, vibrant city came alive with a colorful light show that illuminated the night sky.

The beauty of the city was like nothing else, a magical place where the ancient and modern worlds collide, creating a unique and captivating experience. Amidst absorbing the heavenly beauty of the country, my eyes started searching for my agent, who promised to meet me at Foshan.

After running my eyes across every person that crossed the street, I saw a man walking closer to me with a smile on his face. Finally, I met my agent for the first time. The two strangers, the Chinese agent and I stood in the hallway.

We looked at each other with an unspoken understanding between us. We simultaneously extended our hands and shook. The handshake was a silent agreement between the two of us, a sign of trust in one another.

For the next ten days, I stayed with him in his house, which was much more spacious compared to where I had stayed earlier. He spoke to me in a language that was neither fully English nor Chinese but a strange new hybrid made up of broken syllables, mispronounced words, and stuttering phrases. I replied in kind of a string of words that managed to bridge both cultures, an amalgam of the English language and Indian accent.

He was eager to impart his wisdom, bestowing upon me the gift of language. He was my teacher, illuminating me with the knowledge of the Chinese tongue.

As I listened intently to his guidance, he began to introduce me to the words of a foreign culture. He spoke slowly and clearly so that I could comprehend the complexity of the language. The syllables were foreign to me, yet I felt an eagerness to learn more.

Together, we forged a connection through the exchange of words, and I felt privileged to learn from him. With every word I understood, I felt my understanding of the language grow. I was on my way to gaining an understanding of a whole new world.

However, I was not there to learn a new language but to do something that could make my business take off. The next day, he took me to several popular furniture destinations in China, including Shunde, which is known as the furniture capital of China.

NO MONEY? NO PROBLEM!

    He introduced a lot of stunning wooden products to me, which I saw for the first time in my entire life. I was excited to have seen and touched those things. I picked a few things up, like statues and idols, and placed them on my palm to look at them carefully. The detailing was commendably spectacular.

    I placed them back without dropping them and looked at them again from a little distance. I inquired of the Chinese vendor the cost of his product, yet his words were as inscrutable as a riddle. His speech was a maelstrom of syllables, a cacophony of consonants and vowels, the meaning of which I could not decipher.

    I stood there, dumbfounded, unable to comprehend the vendor's response. Yet, within a few days, I had picked up a few keywords, enough to form a bridge between us.

    I soon learned the power of "hao," used to express appreciation, and the importance of "bu yong xie," a polite way to decline. I also learned the word "xie xie," which means "Thank You." With each phrase, I felt my confidence swell as my comprehension of the language grew.

    It was a beautiful thing to be able to communicate with the people of this foreign land, allowing me to make meaningful connections with the locals. As I continued to learn more words, I felt my bargaining skills sharpen, and I prepared to face whatever the market had in store.

But it is a fact that an Indian like me who spoke broken English could not speak Chinese fluently like a native. I knew that I could not completely understand what they were trying to tell me; therefore, I always kept with me a calculator to convert the currencies and determine whether anything was too expensive or not.

Within ten days, I purchased products to fill up two containers. I was hoping to receive all of them without damage and soon returned to India.

Maheshwari was over the moon as she saw me after so many days. She said she felt those ten days felt longer than ten months. I sat with the family and narrated the whole experience of the journey to them.

They were surprised, nervous, happy, and proud of me, all at the same time. Within a few days, the containers were delivered to our warehouse near Kammanahalli, only to make us realize that those forty-foot containers were bigger than our warehouse.

As the containers moved through the road to reach our warehouse, several electric lines on the roadside broke, leading to a power cut in the locality.

Mathan looked at me with his eyebrows pointing toward the center of his forehead to show his nervousness as people started talking about the damage that happened to the walls and posts nearby.

I looked at him and slowly blinked my eyes in a consoling manner to assure him that we would fix it no matter what happened. After all, we can't send it back or leave it behind. It was a Diwali night, my first Diwali after the wedding, which made it more auspicious.

While Maheshwari waited for me with well-lit diyas all around the house to burst the crackers we bought the previous day, Mathan and I had to go to the warehouse to stack the goods that had just arrived. However, she never complained about my absence that day as she knew how important it was for me to run this business. She had the ability to realize that I was not doing it for myself but for the whole family.

Even though she was not there with me through my childhood, she knew and understood everything really well from my point of view. All she asked me on the night of Diwali was to go to the warehouse confidently and deal with everything with courage. She used to say that nothing could ever defeat a man who has the willpower to convert adversities into opportunities.

She believed that I possessed unique abilities and said that she would never have dared to do so many things, things that I had done as a youngster. She narrates this story to our kids whenever we sit together and talk about where we come from, and I used to feel so happy to see how my kids hugged me tight every time they heard this story. Now, what actually makes me even happier is the fact that my kids are also trying to be like their father. I could see the spark in all their eyes.

We reached the warehouse in no time. But that was the first time we received truckloads of goods at a time. Little did we young brothers know how to arrange things inside a warehouse. Our lack of expertise caused a lot of damage as twenty percent of the products, especially the ones made of glass, were broken. Glass articles in a warehouse should be arranged with care and consideration.

Shelves should be kept dusted and clear of debris to prevent breakage. Labels should be affixed to each shelf to provide an intuitive, organized system of organization. Careful consideration should be given to the placement of heavier items on lower shelves, lighter ones on higher, and fragile pieces cocooned in bubble wrap and softly nestled in the middle. Each article should be lovingly placed with a sense of reverence for the beauty of the glass and the intent to keep it safe and secure.

We were not aware of this, so we kept things one above the other and even heavier things on the top, which eventually broke a number of beautiful articles. Well, since positivity was in the blood, we took it in an optimistic way- only twenty percent was damaged, and eighty percent is still perfect, solid, and magnificent! After all, in the initial stages of the import business, we kept receiving damaged goods, and this time, we realized that we could do it flawlessly on our own. What we lacked was the knowledge about the art of stacking them. We were so ready to learn a new skill and continue to travel across the globe to bring fortune to our country.

If I hadn't taken the bold decision to fly to China, I would still be sitting here waiting for my agent in Chennai to bring the goods in the same old damaged condition. I would have been sitting there fixing and repairing the missing parts like a jigsaw puzzle. What you must understand is the fact that you are your savior. Nobody would come to you and give you a hand to get up from your financial loss as you start a business. It is you who must have the fire within yourself to be daring enough to do the toughest things that people would normally consider impossible.

Takeaway:

Instead of focusing on your limitations, focus on improving your skills every single day. I did not know how to speak Chinese, however, I still managed to get my work done only because I was ready to observe things and stay focused on my goals. I faced betrayal which shattered me entirely, but I still rose stronger than before.

The tunnel might be dark in the beginning, but as you keep moving forward, you will finally find a ray of hope.

Vishruti (Vijai's daughter)

I know that my father and his family lived a pretty hard life from the stories and experiences my father has shared with me about his life. And I know that it's not any easier now. But it is definitely better than before. I really don't think I would even be able to endure all the pain and difficulties my dad had to go through if I were in his place. Considering the personal experiences that I have had, I wouldn't want to live that life ever again. But the best part is that, even through all the hardships, my father did get out of it as if it were nothing at all. And I am delighted that they are living a pretty successful life now. As a matter of fact, I feel like everybody must go through some experience to get to where they want to be in life. But even then, I don't think I would be able to or even want to go through what they went through.

Dad gave us a beautiful life, and I feel lucky to be his daughter. Thinking from a practical perspective, I guess if I were in his shoes, I would not have had the courage to deal with it, but still, if the situation demanded, I would push myself as much as I could and come out as a successful woman. Because, like my dad, I dream pretty big, and even I want to be successful in life no matter what. If I were to live a tough life like that of his, I would definitely build something for myself to get out of the situation that my dad was in because he came from a village. And they basically had nothing. They had to start everything from scratch, but in the end, they succeeded in life.

Although my father and I don't have so many common traits that we share, I believe that we could possibly have the same personalities. As his eldest daughter, I feel like I have a similar personality to him because we have frequent conversations, and the best part is we talk like friends. And I can see how it is just between the two of us without anybody else in between or around. He talks about how he is in this position right now and how much he had to go through to build his identity and many such things. It is beautiful how we never get tired of each other, even if we keep repeating the same stories every day. I want to become like him one day. Even though I'm not in a very bad position, like he was in, I also want to make a living for myself. Although my father has provided everything for me, I still wish to come out as a successful individual, and in that way, I think we are similar.

My father never misses a single chance he gets to spend with us. To make those moments special, we engage in some fun activities. We used to play golf on Sundays for more than two and a half hours. But I just took a break recently since my board exams are around the corner. My father used to say that no matter how rich or poor you are, what earns you respect is a proper education, and for this reason, I have never compromised my academics. I know how hard it was for my dad to balance his business and education in the 1990s. Now that I have all the facilities, the least I have to do is concentrate on my studies. We used to spend a lot of time together before, but now it happens a little less than before. We used to wake up early in the morning and meditate every day because my dad is a very spiritual person. But now we have different timings and schedules. I am busy preparing for my boards, so he never disrupts my sleep in the morning. These days, the time we get to spend together is during dinner.

Dad is so hardworking, and so are his three children. My siblings, too, even though they are too young, work really hard to achieve their goals. All of us are hard-working in our own ways. Whatever we want to accomplish or whatever passions we have, I feel like we put in a lot of effort until we actually get through it. We want to be sincere in everything we do. My brothers, Vihaan and Vivaan, are just fifteen and nine years old, respectively, and they are too young to reveal their personalities. However, I believe that as they grow up, they will turn out to be just like my father, with the same thirst for success and the same sparkle in their eyes to do something great in their lives.

My father inspires me a lot because I have my own father figure in front of my eyes, who had nothing in his pockets but climbed the career ladder successfully to be able to provide everything for us right now. He has taught me to never give up on anything I really desire. Because there will always be obstacles, but after the storm, you accomplish what you aim for. My dad has always been like that, and I can't wait to grow up and look back to my childhood only to realize and reflect back that I have followed my dad's footprints really well.

I think Royaloak is doing really well because it is built upon a strong base made up of hard work, perseverance, honesty, and, of course, determination. As far as I know, my dad and his team are putting in a lot of hard work to make the company better every year. Although I am not aware of the deep insights, through the looks of it, I feel like it's doing really well, and I can actually see how much work they are putting in. Because sometimes, when they get on meetings and calls, I used to be around, and I used to listen well, and I see how they engage and how well everything is coordinated. I also have a clear picture of how serious everyone is about the growth of Royaloak.

I believe that my father has the superpower to transform all the odds into possibilities. I realized this fact when the pandemic kicked in when most people around the globe went into depression and had to go through a state of failure in their careers. Of course, it was a shock because I don't think any of us have gone through something like that before. For my dad, it wasn't good in the start, but I feel like he took that as an advantage to using online business more efficiently. I saw him every day, sitting in one place and working for at least six to seven hours straight. And they barely had any breaks because, obviously, everyone was going through a loss for some time because of COVID. However, I am proud of the way they took that circumstance as an advantage to improve the online field of business. He has proved that having real ambition will take a person to unexpected heights no matter how hard the situation becomes.

My dream is to become an entrepreneur. And hopefully, I even want to have a company of my own in the future. I want to become an independent individual just like my parents, and even I have big goals to chase. I hope I will achieve it one day because my father's story is something that has always inspired me to chase my dreams, and I am working towards fulfilling them. What I'm passionate about is the fashion industry, and I do want to do something in the clothing business. But I would definitely want to be part of Royaloak in the future. I'm not sure in which field, but of course, I would want to be part of it because my dad is putting in a lot of effort. I believe it wouldn't be fair if I were not a part of it because I know that it is only because of Royaloak that we are surviving today. But at the same time, I also want to pursue my own passions, and my parents are so supportive.

We share an uncountable number of beautiful memories. Even though he was busy building Royaloak, he had never forgotten to be with his children during all the important phases of their childhood. I would say that I have the world's best father. There have been a number of events that I will never forget in my entire life. Here is one such story. It was nine years back when my mom had just delivered my youngest brother. Both of my brothers and my mom were at my grandmother's place because mom wanted her mother to take care of her. My dad and I were alone at our house. I was too young to understand the situation, and therefore, I felt lonely because no one else was there for me to play with. My dad, before I even had to speak my feelings out loud, took me out for a drive. He drove me somewhere far away from home to get me an ice gola (shaved ice) every day for one whole week just because he knew how much I loved it as a child. This memory is something that will be stuck with me forever and ever. That is how my father is. He never disappoints anyone. All that he knows is to love and make everyone happy.

When I first spoke to my dad about my ambition of becoming a fashion entrepreneur, he never said no to it. But he gave me the best advice ever. Although I wanted to go to a fashion college, both my parents wanted me to first do a business major and then pursue fashion. Initially, this advice didn't make any sense to me. But now I realize what made them suggest that idea. They are aware that I wish to become an entrepreneur and want to build my identity in the fashion industry. All they want is to ensure that I become independent, and for that, the best way is first to have a business degree so that I will get to know how to start my journey. For this reason, I will be doing a business major and a fashion minor now. And I think if I want to pursue or explore anything more than the fashion industry in the future, a business degree will help me get through it.

Them being our parents motivates us to become a better version of ourselves every single day. Both of them are really hardworking, and they barely take a break because they're doing all of this hard work for us. I really have to appreciate that, and that's really inspiring because there is definitely a lot of workload, but they never really tend to give up or take a break because they feel lazy or if it's just getting too much. Both of them are so sincere about their goals, and that is one quality I admire the most about my parents. Another thing that I specifically love and would praise nonstop about my father is his leadership skills. He implements this skill in his life every day and has motivated us to be like that, too. He really wants the best for us, and for that reason, he teaches us to become like that. My Chikkappa (Mr.Mathan) is also a person with immense leadership qualities, and I believe it is indeed something they both developed while growing up together and building an organization from scratch.

The entire Royaloak family, at this point, is putting their best into the company to make the brand an international sensation, and I am sure that in the upcoming decade, Royaloak furniture will be a part of every single household in the whole wide world. It will definitely hold a lot more value than it does now because my dad keeps talking about it every single day. It will hold a much better reputation than what it has right now; of course, it does have a really good reputation right now. But I feel like it will do so much better in the years that are yet to come. I'm planning to pursue my education in the US, and I am looking forward to the day when I will be buying a piece of furniture for my room from Royaloak's store in the USA. It is also a fact that I can actively support the US branch in growing wider using my knowledge in the field of business. Dad would be so proud of me when he gets to know that his daughter is running the business flawlessly.

I do have a message for my dear, darling dad. I would love to appreciate him for the hard work he's putting in, which then benefits us in a very sophisticated way because he never really makes us go through the things that they went through. With his hard work and sweat, he made sure that we got a better life. I would also love to let him know that he has successfully taught us about what it takes to reach our own personal goals.

I am proud of my dad. I want him to keep going and never stop dreaming big because of the background he has come from. There is no one in this universe who makes me happy other than my father. He is the best in the whole world, and I wish God would gift every child with a father like mine: a man who is courageous, inspires his children, and, moreover, a man who only knows the language of love.

8

SEEDS OF SUCCESS: PLANTING THE FOUNDATIONS FOR GROWTH

"What do you need to start a business? Three simple things: know your product better than anyone, know your customer, and have a burning desire to succeed."

–Dave Thomas, Founder, Wendy's

In the year 2010, I laid the cornerstone of Royaloak. As fortunes smiled upon us, we proudly opened five stores in 2016. Yet, what truly dazzled me was the meteoric rise of our distribution empire, soaring to unprecedented heights.

People usually don't venture into retail when they already have a flourishing distribution network. However, guided by intuition pulsating from within, I sensed that the path to my aspirations lay in retail expansion. With firm faith in my instincts, I chose to take risks of every hue, anticipating the fortune that awaited on the other side.

Just as Dave Thomas said, all that a person requires to start a business, no matter what the age is, is to have an idea about the kind of business they are passionate about and then to strive for satisfaction from every single customer. However, the most important part is to have a strong and fixed ambition. Becoming an entrepreneur is not overnight magic.

You would never find tutorials on how to succeed easily because success never comes with shortcuts. Success is undoubtedly an outcome of various trials and errors.

The story began with a single spark of ambition that burned in my heart as a humble young man who had no money to his name, to whom the odds of success seemed overwhelming. I stood against all the odds and refused to be deterred. I had a dream, and I was determined to make it come true.

I had not even, in a fraction of a moment, thought that my future would be as bright as it is right now. Little did I know my name would one day show up on Google search.

When our decision to expand from selling TV stands to establishing a comprehensive furniture business took shape, we experienced a remarkable upliftment from challenging situations to a point where we could comfortably meet our basic needs.

At the outset, when we ventured into the tea powder business, we held hopes that it would provide some relief for the family during hard times. However, that did not happen the way we wanted it to. But I was not upset about it.

Not even once did I weep over the situation because I always believed that a door closes only when there are some hidden open doors and that you would find it only once you look for it carefully.

Every tragedy, every misery, and every misfortune come under an invisible gift wrap, which gets revealed only after the universe is convinced that we are working hard and well enough.

I made my way to the secret door within a few years, only to realize that I could succeed if I were willing to experiment with a new thing, which eventually led to the exhibition business.

That started moving forward and kept on giving us hope for a better tomorrow. I had to go through the worst times of my life when the exhibitions at Kannur and Mysore became intricate. But I was not taken aback.

I knew that I had to show courage where it was necessary. It would not have made sense if I gave up due to the inconvenient circumstances and regretted it later.

Finally, when we began selling TV stands, everything started to change, marking the beginning of a new dawn. It took absolutely less time to construct each frame compared to the time we used to roam around in markets to purchase other, more minor things.

Slowly, the exhibition business became OAK and OAK, a new furniture store.

I strongly believe that when you have a positive intent, everything will fall into place. The right people will automatically come closer to you – helping you in the larger scheme of things. You may not realize it at that point, but eventually you do. During this juncture, a young customer walked into Oak & Oak along with his wife to buy a TV stand. At the billing section, he saw our product leaflet next to the billing desk, and he enquired with the sales executive, "Who designed this leaflet? It is not doing justice to the brand and its offerings".

He left his number with the sales executive and said he would be happy to assist with the brand communications for Oak & Oak. His name is Riju Kolurathil Paulose, and he is a highly creative professional who has worked in top advertising agencies in India and UAE.

He somehow felt that Oak & Oak as a brand had not reached its audience purely due to ineffective design and communication; he firmly believed that the brand had the potential to grow further as the products were genuinely priced and had something for everyone who walked into the store.

After a few days, I met Riju, who later made an interesting leaflet that changed the brand's identity altogether. Later, when I asked him to work on the new logo for Royaloak, he came out with not only some brilliant design options but also with a tagline that read, "Discover Style, at Honest Prices." The tagline resonated with Oak & Oak's honest approach.

He is the one who created the Royaloak leaf logo and slowly educated me on the importance of investing efforts in proper brand communication. Because, at the end of the day, no matter how good the product offering is, if the messaging does not reach the audience, it won't garner any long-term returns.

He told me that every piece of design or communication is a micro-investment toward building a strong brand.

Today, I am happy for his 14-plus years of association with Royaloak as creative director. Somehow, I had a feeling that this young man had good vibes and always had an interesting take on things when it came to brand building.

We were looking forward to developing Oak & Oak back then, which was when we were asked to change the name.

A stranger from Chennai asked us to go for an alternate name and claimed that he had already registered the same name for his company.

He was apparently expecting us to bribe him with a handsome amount, but to his bad luck, we agreed to forget the old name and find a new one.

He, in reality, lied to us for monetary benefit. By 2010, Oak & Oak changed to Royaloak as we realized that branding and premiumization were of utmost importance.

But today, when I look back, I believe that that man was sent to me by the universe. It was indeed a blessing in disguise. It was after changing the name to Royaloak that we actually started making a mark in the industry. Everything in life happens for a reason, and therefore, it is essential to embrace everything, be it sorrow or happiness. We changed the name of all three outlets to Royaloak. We designed a logo for the company, and every time I looked at the name board on top of the stores, a different kind of energy rushed through my veins, only to make me realize how far I had come. Hard work always pays off in the end.

The most challenging part of my entrepreneurial journey is that, unlike other businesses, we never had an investor. When every other organization had wealthy people investing money, Royaloak was blessed with just five thousand rupees that our mother gave us in the beginning. As I always say, she is the only god I know, and it is indeed because of her love that we are where we are right now. It is nothing less than a herculean task to build a venture from scratch. We kept on investing all the savings back into the business until we could have a significant return on the investment. After the year 2010, we saw that our lives were changing in unexpected ways. In the meantime, we introduced more products to the clan. People started talking about the superior quality of our TV stands and other types of furniture, and we saw a massive number of items getting sold out in a short span. It started to get a bit difficult for us to manage the sales and finances simultaneously. At this point, we were capable of hiring people to speed up our processes. Gradually, we started growing from a one-person show into an entire organization. This is how growth happens- the process might look slow, but success would surely follow. Like someone once said, "slowly, but surely" is a quote that has always inspired me. We eventually added more and more members to the growing family, and in the end, we had a pack of wolves in the team who pushed themselves to bring great results to the organization. People asked me how I was going to cover the salaries of the newly hired teammates. I was not anxious about that, for I was sure if there was a will, there was certainly a way. The headcount started to increase day by day, and things started getting a lot easier for us in terms of management.

Several people came up with questions regarding the name of the organization. Since I was growing by leaps and bounds day by day, they suggested that it would be better if I named the company after my family name. But I was totally against this notion- business and family are not supposed to be mixed up ever. When I looked at the most successful organizations worldwide, I happened to figure out that none of them have named their companies after their names, starting from Reliance to Infosys. A business is where money keeps coming and going. You can revive it from any stage using money, but family is something that money can't buy. It is a connection that you can never find anywhere. I was not ready to mix them up at any cost. Ever since childhood, I only worked to provide my family with a better lifestyle, and for that, I never wanted to compare or blend my family life with anything under the sky.

As Royaloak started to grow to become a massive tree with strong roots, there came a need to keep increasing the quality of the products consistently. Customer reviews were everything to us. If you take a closer look, you will understand that we have never used celebrities to promote our brand. Our fame came in through word-of-mouth marketing. We provided the best quality products at the lowest price in the market to our customers, and with that, the number of people who trusted us kept skyrocketing. The best part is that most of our products were internationally imported ones. Can you imagine buying a German-made dining table set for the price of a regular dining set? No, right? But that is possible at Royaloak, and that is what made us top the list of South India's best furniture companies and, later, India's number one furniture company. I kept calling the store managers every day to get lists of comments given by our customers to ensure that they were satisfied. We trained our crew members on a regular basis to make them the perfect fit for the store and every single customer. There were and still are other companies that provide international products, but I was not at all worried about the competition.

Worrying about competitors is the biggest negative thought an entrepreneur could ever have. I never let this thought come near me. The world is wide enough to provide opportunities for everyone to prove their worth. I believe nature is equally kind to every one of us. All of us are equally blessed with twenty-four hours a day, and it all depends upon how well we use it. Resources are equally available to all the eight billion people on the planet. Learning to utilize them wisely is what makes a person successful. I could have lived my childhood in complete sorrow, but growing up in a place like Munnar and not making use of the tea estates would have made me look stupid in front of the world. I took the plunge to develop it, and that is precisely how we grew to become leaders in our specialized industry, and that is exactly why we are at this stage where we have more than two hundred physical stores of Royaloak across south India, bringing us a fortune every day. Yes, we have come across so much criticism from different sides, some blaming the decisions that I make, some from the customers who got their products delivered delayed due to unavoidable situations, and many such incidents. However, what still kept us going forward was our open-minded approach toward everything.

Communication is the key to any relationship. I had a dedicated team who were willing to contact the unhappy customers to understand their problems and resolve them with immediate effect.

They also contacted other happy customers to inform them about the new product launches and the best offers.

As the number of stores kept increasing, we decided to bring it to a franchisee setup so that the profit would be increased, and with that, we could have many more people to share the profit with. It is important to understand that we need people around us for everything: to support, to criticize, to correct, and to share. This completes our purpose. Whatever we earn becomes more priceless when we share it with others. Our Kammanahalli store was as small as a cardboard box with just eight hundred square feet of area. We sold a couple of sofas and, later on, expanded the number of items by adding bean bags, dining table sets, and many more things to the list. Later on, we opened another store at CMH road in Indira Nagar Bangalore with an area of hardly two thousand square feet and another one in Marathahalli with another two thousand square feet area which we had constructed using our funds rather than taking for rent. It ran successfully, and soon, we pooled up enough savings to build our fourth showroom at Banaswadi with an area of over twenty thousand square feet, which eventually turned out to be our head office. This was a moment when the younger version of myself was so proud of himself and his family.

We saw our biggest sale during the Diwali season. Our total target was five million. But to our surprise, we managed to earn our target profit within just one day, leaving us all in a state of jubilation. It called for a huge celebration.

If you are young and planning to become an entrepreneur, remember that your goal should not be to make more money; rather, it must be woven into a vision. It could be anything, such as helping society or improving the lifestyles of the people around you. Always remember that age is just a number. All you must have is a real vision rather than a selfish need.

When Royaloak started becoming a name, our purpose was to provide international quality products to the ordinary people in our country at affordable prices. When your vision is authentic and sensible, everything starts to fall into place.

What is more important than money is humanity, spirituality, and honesty. It would be best if you cultivated a positive mindset, and that is what will help you become a better person. Another thing that helped me was my discipline. Your mind is just like a sponge early in the morning. It absorbs everything that is being poured onto it, and hence, it is essential to wake up early and practice something that could help you, such as workouts or yoga and meditation. Remember to pour good things onto it. With this, your mind becomes clear and devoid of negative thoughts, and it will work as fuel to keep you running throughout the entire day. Trust your intuitions, no matter what comes in between.

There is no need to calculate your finances if your vision is strong enough. Because nothing grows in the right direction if you are skeptical about growth, and calculating finances will adversely affect your confidence, and you may deter yourself from taking much-needed risks in your business. Every time I thought about finances, my mind kept whispering, "Everything will be fine. Just go on. All you need to do is to trust yourself and your intuitions." You have to do it; everything else will follow.

I believe that there are two ways to worship God. The first one is by meditating all day without working on anything else, and the other one is by meditating for a while to clear your mind and step out of your house to do something good for society. Krishna's wisdom to Arjuna in the Bhagavad Gita shows paths to connect with the divine: the reflective path of Jnana Yoga and the selfless action of Karma Yoga. The lesson isn't a choice between praying endlessly or engaging in warfare; rather, it's about understanding that both paths can lead to spiritual fulfillment.

Society's improvement becomes the ultimate reward when we wholeheartedly dedicate our actions, regardless of our chosen path, to the betterment of the world. Thus, whether in prayerful solitude or amidst the fray of duties, the key lies in selflessly contributing to society's upliftment as a pathway to the divine. I realized that the more I contributed some positivity to the people around me, the more I received blessings in different ways. Every time you do something good, more people will benefit. That way, your life will become meaningful. My life has had a purpose ever since I was a little boy. I wanted to improve my family life as well as provide affordable products to ordinary people so that they can also enhance their lives. I worked hard, and the end result was stunning. I was always very disciplined in my life, taking things slow and never rushing. I knew that I had to take my time and learn from my mistakes rather than just running through life, never looking back. This has helped me to stay focused on the crucial things and not be overwhelmed by the small stuff. Even when something wrong happens, I remind myself that everything will be okay. I remember, during my teenage years, I had often seen people getting frustrated by the most trivial things, but I learned that this was a waste of energy. Every time I felt like a bad thing was approaching, I shifted my focus onto the positive and found solutions to the problems I faced. I learned that I could use my discipline and knowledge to overcome any obstacle in life, no matter how difficult it seemed.

Nature has an answer for everything. I look outside whenever I get the feeling of an unknown hurricane approaching to devour my peace of mind; the music of the free-flowing lakes and the chirping and chattering of birds and raindrops have a splendid healing effect, and they have answers for all my questions. It is essential to recognize the joys of life that can be found in the smallest of moments, from the warmth of a gentle embrace to the melodious sounds of a songbird to the simple pleasure of a deep breath of fresh air. Finding happiness in these little things is what makes life so precious.

A manifestation is a tool like Brahmastra; nature provides you with everything through the power of manifestation. If you ask for money or discipline or positivity, you receive it almost in an instant. I have always sought to live with a purity of soul, honoring the highest level of integrity. Through this commitment, I have found strength and beauty that brings richness to my life. With a willingness to remain truthful and honest, I have come to understand the power of this virtue and the peace of mind that accompanies it. Integrity is a choice that has become part of my identity, a way of life that I will forever embrace.

One thing I always kept in mind was that I must only take one step at a time rather than grabbing it all at once. The first thing to a successful entrepreneurial journey is to fix a vision and fix what product to showcase. Once that is sorted, one must think about opening a shop. When Mathan and I realized that furniture was our niche, we opened a store and then decided what name to give it. After we figured that out, we decided what color to paint the interior of our dream venture. That is how things must work. A billion-dollar business can be started from scratch just the way Royaloak started from tiny plastic articles at local exhibition stalls. We worked hard to make it a success. We never expected anything from anywhere or anyone. We took life as it came without any disagreement or disappointment. Had I kept my expectations high, I would have become a person with uncontrollable anger issues and would have eventually deviated from my path of spirituality and success. Positivity is the ultimate recipe for success, both in personal life as well as in business.

Tiruvalluvar, a famous Tamil poet, once said, *"You must always show others the same things and services that you yourself desire."* If you wish to buy affordable products, give that to your customers; if you expect loyalty from others, be loyal to your customers; if you think you require a larger quantity of products, provide the same for your customers. If you feel you need the best quality products, give them the best quality products. This way, we gained more customers, and it helped us increase the profit in the long run.

The potency of our minds is extraordinary. It is of utmost importance to nourish it with nothing but positive musings. Our minds are like gardens, and we are the gardeners. By filling it with inspiring and uplifting thoughts, we can cultivate a garden of bliss and contentment. One single negative thought can be like an invisible worm; it could eat up the entire garden without you even getting a chance to notice it. You may again get pushed back to zero, the place where it all began.

I had to go through a number of devastating moments, but the only thing that kept me going was the positivity in me, which I never let go of. Now, when I look at where I came from, all I can see is a boy with an empty pocket climbing a tall ladder toward success. The entrepreneur title is not just a fancy title but a whole difficult task and indeed a responsibility towards the entire world.

I never looked for hope outside of myself, for I had an inner light that would never go out. Even when money was slipping through my pocket like water, I stayed calm and positive. My faith in myself was unshakable, and I knew that I could create something special, something that would make a mark in the world. And so, I began my journey.

I worked tirelessly to make a name for myself, and slowly, I began to see the fruits of my labor. With a little bit of luck, I was able to build my own company, Royaloak, and over time, it became renowned as one of the best furniture brands in India. I had come a long way from where I had started, and I never lost sight of my goal.

I continued to strive for excellence, and with each passing day, I could feel my hopes and dreams slowly becoming a reality. I worked hard to make sure that my company was the best it could possibly be, and it paid off in the end.

I knew that I had succeeded in fulfilling my vision when I saw the look of joy and satisfaction on the faces of my customers. I knew exactly what my customers were looking for, and I ensured that they got everything before stepping out of the store.

They had put their trust in me, and I had not let them down. I had my family and my cousins by my side all the time, who directly and indirectly helped me grow in my career and taught me how to deal with customers and other people. I had a lot of ups and downs in my entire journey, but what kept me going was the right type of people that I was surrounded with.

As COVID-19 infiltrated every nook and cranny of the world, we made a bold decision to rise above the challenges and forge ahead. Determined to weather the storm, we worked tirelessly for several days and nights, channeling our unwavering resolve into the growth of our enterprise. The fruits of our labor soon became evident as Royaloak swiftly established seventy-five stores, which was fifty before, within three months.

Undeterred by obstacles, we set our sights higher, embarking on an ambitious endeavor to secure an additional seventy stores. Yet, despite our best efforts, circumstances dictated that only forty-five of these could be opened. Nevertheless, a glimmer of hope illuminated our path. Within six months of the lockdown being eased, Royaloak proudly opened a hundred stores across South India, solidifying our position as India's #1 furniture brand.

What propelled us on this remarkable journey? It was a potent blend of courage, the willingness to take risks, and the unwavering commitment of our outstanding teammates. Their dedication formed the bedrock of our success, breathing life into our aspirations and propelling us forward.

The year 2016 stands as a testament to the resilience we cultivated. A period of immense challenge and uncertainty unfolded as the government implemented restrictions and unfavorable policies for import business, seemingly tilting the scales against us. it was as if a train moving in full speed came to a sudden forceful halt. It was a shock to all of us. The system appeared to favor businesses with substantial investments, leaving us, a company that had started from humble beginnings, in a state of extreme distress.

Overwhelmed and disheartened, I contemplated closing the doors of our enterprise by retaining just two stores. This means eighty percent of our business would go down the drain.

With a heavy heart, I confided in Maheshwari, Mathan, and Preethi, sharing my agonizing decision. Together, we mustered the courage to address our staff members, fully anticipating that they would go in search of greener pastures. To my astonishment, however, a stirring display of loyalty and solidarity unfolded before my eyes.

Over a hundred members from our team approached me, their voices trembling with emotion, pleading to preserve Royaloak. Tears glistened in their eyes as they implored me not to shutter the company that had become their livelihood. I couldn't sleep for four days in a row. Their genuine concern touched the depths of my soul, for I realized that our existence held profound significance in their lives.

These individuals, whose children attended nearby private schools and whose homes were situated in close proximity to our office, relied on Royaloak for sustenance. Relocating to another organization would have entailed tremendous hardship and upheaval for them. That was a point in my life where I realized that my life had a vast and meaningful purpose. It was in that transformative instant that I realized that my purpose extended far beyond mere commerce. My duty was to provide for these hundreds of individuals and their families who had placed their trust in Royaloak. Ninety-five percent of our team worked for a really long time with us, and only five percent left the company in a year or two. The majority were committed to the work they were doing. Their faces were etched in my memory, and I could not fathom abandoning them. Our lives, I realized, are intertwined with a greater calling—to nourish and uplift those who rely on us.

I couldn't bear to see their tears. The four directors of Royaloak, Mathan, Preethi, Maheshwari, and I sat down for a long discussion. We decided to go into aggressive expansion mode in order to make things better for our workforce in 2017.

Ever since then, I never had to, not in a fraction of a second, think about wrapping up our business. But, yes, we had to reduce the number of stores we had in order to survive the governmental policies. Soon, Royaloak LLP was upgraded to Royaloak Incorporation Private Limited.

Haven't you heard about ikigai? It is indeed a profound philosophy that guides individuals in discovering their true passions, values, and purpose. Interestingly, as fate would have it, it was during the critical juncture when Royaloak's future hung in the balance that I myself came to realize the power of my own ikigai.

Now, if we cast our gaze back upon the remarkable growth trajectory of Royaloak post-2016, prepare to be enthralled by the remarkable tale that unfolds. Picture a peacock gracefully rising from the ground, spreading its vivid wings, breathing life into a brand that defied all odds. In 2017, our team wanted to make Royaloak the number one furniture company in Bangalore. As a result of their support and our teamwork, we managed to open ten stores, and the vibrant city of Bangalore proudly crowned us as its number one furniture brand — a testament to our unwavering commitment and exceptional craftsmanship.

The spirit to come out victorious is a quality that everyone at Royaloak possesses. The following year, they were determined to bring out Royaloak as Karnataka's best furniture company. All of us worked day and night to turn this wish into reality. We opened twenty more stores across Karnataka, and towards the end of the year, we had a total of thirty stores across the state. The entire state of Karnataka stood in awe as we claimed the coveted title of its number-one furniture brand that year.

In the year 2019, fueled by insatiable ambition, our gaze extended far beyond the horizons of achievement. Our grand vision? To dominate the vast expanse of South India. Across the southern landscape, twenty-five Royaloak stores emerged, their stature imposing and their allure undeniable. Cities like Chennai and Hyderabad bore witness to the majestic presence of our establishments, standing tall amidst the bustling urbanity and the serene towns alike. With unwavering resolve, our tally reached an impressive fifty-five stores, a testament to our unrelenting pursuit of excellence in the southern reaches of the country. The applause echoed through the southern skies as we claimed the coveted title of the unrivaled number-one brand in South India. The air was thick with jubilation, and our aspirations soared higher, fueled by the collective cheers of an entire region. Alas, just as victory seemed within our grasp, as you already know, the world was thrust into the clutches of the relentless COVID-19 pandemic.

Yet, true to the indomitable spirit that defines Royaloak, we refused to yield. With unbeatable resolve, we navigated through the strongest storm, adapting and evolving in the face of unprecedented challenges. We booked another seventy stores in different parts of the country. But we could open only fifty. And lo and behold, in 2021, against all odds, we emerged triumphant, fulfilling our destiny as India's foremost furniture brand with 100+ stores, and today, in 2024, we have 200+stores. With that, we earned a lot of fame and wealth.

As you already know, money is an invaluable asset. However, I had the sense to understand that money is not everything in life. Sometimes, it is the determination that matters. And in the end, it is always hard work that wins us every title.

The initiation of any business is the result of the business owner's determination. However, as time goes by, what makes an entrepreneur successful is their customers and supporters. I am blessed enough to have millions of happy customers around me and it is a pleasure to see people recognizing me out of the crowd as Vijai Subramaniam, Founder of Royaloak.

Takeaway:

Life is a beautiful journey; as you go forward, make sure you're helping others. The true purpose of your life must be to genuinely care for the entire humankind. I wanted my employees to be happy. The moment I realized they need my support, I decided to refrain from closing the doors of our organization. Finally, with their support Royaloak became India's #1 furniture company. Team work coupled with dedication and hard work lets you achieve anything in life.

Suresh Bava (interview done in Kannada)

Vijai is my brother's best friend, and I first met him in the year 2000. We developed a great bond within a short period of time. I could only think of Vijai as an extremely hard-working individual who has the courage to do anything and everything. The more I saw him working, and the more I saw his interest in the work he has been doing, the more I knew that Vijai would rule Bangalore one day. I had once casually told him the same in a not-so-serious manner, but now, it seems like my predictions have come true. When we first met, he was doing a little business that did not bring him a huge profit the way it is happening now, but he was really happy and confident.

Vijai is a complete family man. After work, he drives home as fast as he can because he cannot think of wasting a single moment that he could spend with his beautiful family. He never travels without his family, and it is really good to see that they share an amazing bond. Apart from being a great husband and father, he is also a humble person who is willing to help and support others in the society of which he is a part. Even now, after being well settled in life, he doesn't have an attitude problem; he is never arrogant or complacent and will talk to everybody without any bias. He is quite accommodating in nature; he takes only the positive side of everything, even if we talk to him about something negative.

Vijai has been a joyful person since childhood, and he has always been really helpful. Now, he has become even more helpful. He is so obsessed with positivity and a positive environment. He says I am the person who helped and supported him in setting up the Royaloak store in Bangalore. But I think it is his determination that took him to this level. I supported him because I could see that spark of confidence in his eyes. He had a fire in him from the very beginning, and I could see that clearly. I knew that he would achieve greater things in life. It's been 23 years since we have been preserving our friendship, and to this day, I have never seen a negative thing in Vijai.

When Vijai opened the first store for Royaloak, nobody knew the brand. Nobody knew who Vijai was. But he still kept working. As the first store started performing well, Vijai opened 2 to 3 more shops at a time. At that point, I was sure that he would soon be able to launch 25+ stores, and surprisingly, the prediction did come true within a short period of time. He is performing really well, and I want him to continue the effort. I want life to give Vijai the best of everything. Over four thousand to five thousand families are benefiting from Vijai's success in the form of employment as well as affordable furniture. Although I have been with him right from the beginning of the birth of Royaloak, I would say it is all because of Vijai's positive mindset that the company is being recognized now.

Vijai is a highly disciplined person. He has a fixed routine, and he follows that without fail, and that proves his dedication to the things that he has been doing. I am proud of the person that he has become in all these years. The way he respects everyone is something that has to be appreciated. He never points out the fault in others. If in case the person opposite him has done something wrong, what Vijai does is talk to them calmly and take the first step to fix the issue rather than making it a huge deal, and that is exactly why he is a successful entrepreneur. He is thoughtful and supportive of others and does everything he can to bring a smile to someone else's face.

I believe Vijai, as a human being, deserves more success than what he already has, and one day, the world will recognize him as one of the most successful entrepreneurs of all time and as a family man who is well capable of balancing his personal life and entrepreneur life.

9
SEEING TOMORROW, TODAY

"Good leaders have a vision and inspire others to help them turn vision into reality. Great leaders create more leaders, not followers. Great leaders have a vision, share vision, and inspire others to create their own."
—Roy T. Bennett

What is life without its hardest twists and turns? I would say it is unadventurous and boring. What would you say? Do you think you must live a plain, black-and-white life, absolutely colorless and tiring? Do you feel drawn to explore new horizons and challenge your boundaries to enhance your life's circumstances and achieve greater success, or do you find contentment and fulfillment in the stability and routine of a nine-to-five job?

The beginning of every journey is from a single dot. Like a beacon of light, it beckons us forward, providing the faintest glimmer of hope that our dreams may be realized. It is from this single dot that a successful business is born, as a single grain of sand is the start of a pearl. The words of success seemed so far away when I first started my business. I had no way of predicting the future, no way of knowing whether I'd ever be successful or else fail miserably.

All I had was unending hopes and a dream that I never wanted to give up on, and that was all I had to go on. I set out on a journey into the unknown, a voyage of uncertainty, but I was determined to make it work.

I worked tirelessly, day and night, never once giving up, never once allowing doubts to take hold. I worked hard, and I made sacrifices because without sacrificing and working out of your comfort zone, you would never become successful. I kept my eye on the ultimate goal, like a leopard focusing on its prey deep inside the woods. My journey was not without its struggles and its challenges.

There were instances when I thought I was swimming upstream, and I often had several doubts in my mind related to so many things that I had been doing.

I had never seen a successful entrepreneur at a young age. The only person who became my inspiration was my mother, who spent all her life stacking tiny snacks and foods on the shelves of her small petti-kadai, and to me, she was the first businessperson ever, even though she was not really successful.

One thing that I have adopted from her and still have a hold over is her patience and the attitude of never giving up. Following her example, I, too, refused to give up when hard times kicked in, and I kept pushing myself forward.

Now, after all these years, when I look back, I can't believe how far I have come. I have achieved more than I ever dreamed of, and I am in awe of my own success. The joy of accomplishment is incomparable. It is a feeling that fills my heart with immense pride and joy as I look upon the success of my business. A journey that started with just a tiny seed of an idea has now flourished into an affluent enterprise.

Right at this moment, I am sincerely appreciative of the opportunities I have been granted in life, the people I have in my corner, and the resources I have been given. I believe in the practice of gratitude, and it has helped a lot in my entire journey. The more I practiced gratitude, the greater the positive energy that surrounded me.

From the very beginning, I was nothing more than an impoverished soul with an idea—an idea that could possibly change my life. I was determined to make it happen, no matter the cost. I worked hard for long hours and sacrificed so much of my own comfort and stability.

I took risks that could have cost me everything, but I knew it was worth it. Not only did I want to provide things for myself, but I wanted to be able to create a life that I could be proud of. With each passing day, my hard work started to pay off. I was able to step out of the shadows of poverty and into a life that was more stable. I was able to make a real difference in the lives of those around me. Every exhibition we hosted was extremely risky since we had spent everything we had in our pockets to purchase goods to display at the exhibition ground.

Had it been a failure, we would have had to starve for months in order to make a few hundred rupees to survive for another few days. The first exhibition where I sold garments was undoubtedly a catastrophe and caused me all the funds I had been saving up for months. Even though I kept smiling outside, my heart was wrenching and weeping so hard from the inside, and I was the only person who could hear those silent cries.

Maybe that was all a part of the universe's way of preparing me for something big, or rather, that is what I wanted to believe. I have always been grateful for every single experience that the universe threw at me, be it really good or highly lamentable.

I was never worried or anxious about what the future had in store for me. All I invested in was making the most out of the present. If I could work for twenty hours a day, I would do that rather than regret not doing anything at all.

Time is indeed a gift, a blessing that has the potential to blow up or change your entire life. It is something we all have in common. As I was growing up, I had the sense to realize that N. R. Narayana Murthy and I had the same number of hours a day. If he could build Infosys, why can't a young boy from the rural areas of Tamil Nadu dream of becoming successful one day in the future?

After all, like someone once said, "Always dare to dream. For as long as there's a dream, there is hope, and as long as there is hope, there is joy in living."

Although Royaloak began as a venture that had no future plans and lived totally in the present, we are now planning some things for the betterment of the organization.

Every organization has a life, just like human beings. An organization takes birth and crawls through its childhood just like a human child who crawls on his legs for the first three years. The organization will then grow to embrace its beautiful youth, where it will be obsessed with the way it looks and craves more beauty and improvisation, just like how kids grow up and become conscious about the way they look and try to look beautiful in the mirror.

The only thing that makes an organization different from a human is that human beings will pass away in less than a hundred years, but the organization might live for infinite numbers of years as long as the legacy of the owner is taken forward flawlessly by the successors.

My dream as a child to rescue my family from struggles became accomplished the moment the exhibition business took off.

When you start achieving your littlest dreams one after the other, you become obsessed with the person you become after each winning.

I was fortunate enough to experience the ultimate joy of achieving goals, and with every victory, I got the confidence to dream even more extensively; the canvas kept growing without limits. We are not born to remain stuck in one city or one country; the world is a vast space, and you have to touch every place possible, before life comes to an end.

When we opened our first showroom in Kammanahalli and began to receive a great response, we managed to expand it further. We opened several stores in Karnataka, as it is a huge state where people purchase furniture in large quantities. But the moment we realized that we deserved to explore other states as well, we worked for several months and opened stores in different locations across all the south Indian states.

Success is apparently not a thing that can happen with the touch of a magic wand but is something that requires constant nurturing and polishing.

The more we traveled to other south Indian states and opened our store, the more the organization became improvised. With every new shop, we made sure to add up some more variety of articles so that our customers could have unending options to select from. Although we were growing commendably in the South, we realized that the end goal of every growing organization has to be global growth, no matter how big or small it is. As I always say, everything starts from a dot. The more I looked at the world's most popular brands, the more I understood that everything is possible and the ultimate goal should be not just one country but the entire world. When Starbucks first opened its doors, it could barely contain the aroma of freshly brewed coffee within the confines of a humble coffee shop. But with the passage of time, their popularity grew exponentially, eventually blossoming into the global phenomenon we know today. From the outside, looking in, it's nothing short of a modern-day miracle; it is a shining example of perseverance and hard work paying off in the most remarkable way.

The genesis of Infosys began in a tiny office room at the abode of Narayana Murthy. The journey of this startup, from a small space to a worldwide brand, is undoubtedly evidence of the power of innovation and determination. It is a story of a man's ambition to make a difference and turn a dream into reality. Narayana Murthy's legacy will be passed on as a reminder to future generations of the potential of human ambition and the power of hard work.

These are not the only examples that I could think of. There are a hundred more that I could tirelessly speak about, and at the end of the list, there will be "Royaloak" and Vijai Subramaniam in the next five years, leading the world in commendable ways.

India is an incredible country, a land of sprawling landscapes and vibrant cultures, a place of ancient traditions and captivating beauty, with a diverse array of landscapes stretching from the snow-capped peaks of the Himalayas to the sun-drenched beaches of the South. What makes it even more worthwhile is the fact that each state looks like a whole separate country- it is more like twenty-eight countries within one single country. I wanted Royaloak to be present in all the twenty-eight so-called countries, and as a part of accomplishing this dream, I launched physical stores of our brand in the entire southern region. Later, I conquered many more mini-countries, and right now, I am looking forward to becoming a global leader.

As the business world continues to change and grow, so too must our company. We aspire to lead the way in this global revolution, building bridges between countries, cultures, and markets. To this end, we have set our sights on a five-year plan for global expansion.

In 2020, we won the title of India's best furniture brand, and in the next five years, we aim to become the world's best furniture brand. I aim to increase my management power and prove that an Indian has the ability to conquer the entire planet with his skills. The world has already seen the presence of Indians in every industry.

People like Sundar Pichai and Narayana Murthy have been ruling the world for several decades, and I'm looking forward to being one among them in the years to come. It is a moment of goosebumps to see people from all over the world reporting to Indian leaders. I want the world to remember me as a person who came from a hopeless place and grew up to become one of the most popular global leaders. Upon my birth, I was greeted with laughter, as is customary for many newborns in the world. But I have always wanted my life to be different, something that everyone would remember long after I am gone. All I want right now is to be that inspirational businessman who would leave an everlasting mark on the world.

I happened to realize that I have already made a huge impact on the lives of my teammates. In the pivotal moment when the decision to scale down the business to just two stores was made, the heartache reflected in the eyes of my people stirred a profound awakening within me. It was an epiphany that transcended mere business strategy—it was the revelation of my life's true purpose. Since that poignant juncture, my life's journey has been a narrative of constant evolution, an unwavering commitment to enriching the lives of those who form the very essence of our existence.

From the very core of my being, a commitment surged forth—a dedication to rewriting the narrative of those around me. It wasn't solely about profit margins or market dominance; it was about forging a legacy woven with compassion and empowerment.

Our vision extended beyond the confines of our walls. We endeavored to be architects of opportunity, cultivating robust relationships with our business partners, logistics associates, marketing vendors, and a sprawling network of over 400 factories engaged in crafting Royaloak furniture. It wasn't just about production; it was about fostering a community where every stroke of craftsmanship resonated with livelihoods, both directly and indirectly.

But it didn't end there. With the evolution from an LLP to an incorporation, a new chapter unfolded in our aspirations. Royaloak ceaselessly aspired not just to sell furniture but to encapsulate an experience—an international lifestyle accessible to all at unprecedented prices.

The cornerstone of this ambition lay not solely in business growth but in nurturing a conducive environment where the happiness and well-being of the members of the team are intrinsic to our success.

Beyond the realms of corporate strategies lay a heartfelt desire to be remembered for something far greater than business prowess. It was an aspiration to be etched in the annals of society as a force for positive change, leaving behind a legacy that transcended material success.

The metamorphosis witnessed in the Indian furniture industry stands as a testament to our pursuit. Before Royaloak, customers navigated a landscape of dissatisfaction, settling for lackluster pieces from local stores and resorting to customization out of necessity or, I would say, helplessness. However, to everyone's luck, our arrival heralded a transformative era—a haven where each piece of furniture exuded uniqueness sourced from distant lands like Malaysia, Italy, and America. Our gift to customers was not just furniture; it was an experience—an international aesthetic at prices defying convention, all while upholding uncompromising standards of quality.

However, beyond the realms of commerce lay an unyielding truth—an organization's destiny, akin to a binary code, is simply growth or demise. The growth of Royaloak is intertwined with the aspirations of our teammates. We fostered an ecosystem where career progression wasn't a lofty aspiration but a tangible reality, weaving threads of loyalty and dedication that bound our team to us.

Our mission stands as a testament to a deeper purpose—At the heart of it lies a commitment to the profound happiness of our customers. And when I speak of customers, it's not just the individuals purchasing our products; it encompasses a triad of souls reliant on us for their fulfillment.

The first are the pillars of our foundation—the employees. Beyond merely paying salaries, our dedication to them is rooted in something far deeper. We strive to imbue within them a profound sense of their worth in society. It's about painting a vivid picture, illustrating how their presence isn't just a cog in the wheel but a vital brushstroke in the canvas of the world that, I believe, forms the very bedrock upon which their growth thrives—a nurturing environment that fosters not just professional development but personal fulfillment.

We cultivate a landscape where understanding their significance isn't merely a platitude but a lived reality. It's about creating a nurturing backdrop where they aren't just employees but essential contributors to a collective vision. It's in these moments of realization that seeds of purpose are sown, laying the groundwork for their individual blossoming. After all, a healthy and thriving environment isn't just about the tangible rewards but the intangible—the feeling of being an integral part of a larger picture, contributing to something greater than oneself. For our vendors, we strive to foster relationships that transcend mere business transactions. They are partners in our journey, integral threads woven into the fabric of our success. It's about more than just timely deliveries or favorable terms; it's about cultivating a symbiotic ecosystem where mutual growth and respect thrive. We acknowledge their role as essential contributors, acknowledging their craftsmanship, dedication, and commitment. Their success is intricately entwined with ours, and in nurturing these alliances, we create a tapestry of trust and reliability that withstands the test of time.

And then, there are our esteemed customers—individuals who place their trust in us to fulfill their desires. It's not just about selling products; it's about curating experiences that resonate with their aspirations and dreams. We perceive them not as buyers but as connoisseurs seeking something more—a blend of quality, uniqueness, and affordability. We deliver not just products but moments of delight and satisfaction.

And in the immortal words of Gandhi, customers embody the divine essence of our enterprise. They are the patrons who bless us not just with their purchases but with the very sustenance of our journey. Their currency isn't just money; it's the life force that nourishes our ability to compensate and foster growth. They're the guiding force behind our employees' livelihoods and the impetus driving our expansion. Gandhi's ethos reminds us that the customer isn't just a benefactor; they are the divine architects of our progression, the reason behind our existence, nurturing our ability to not just survive but to thrive and evolve.

Every interaction, every purchase, is an opportunity to elevate their lives, to offer them something exceptional. We understand their needs and aspirations, and we endeavor to offer not just what they seek but what they didn't even know they desired. It's about crafting a journey, a story that begins with their first interaction with our products and continues long after, leaving an indelible imprint of quality, reliability, and contentment.

Our mission, therefore, encapsulates a holistic approach—a commitment to nurturing relationships, fostering growth, and weaving a story of satisfaction and fulfillment for all stakeholders involved, ensuring that each, be it our work force, vendors, or customers, feels valued, empowered, and indispensable to the collective journey we tread together.

Royaloak would grow larger and soon become an incomparable and fantastic furniture brand from which the world would shop. We are aiming to make products that are affordable to everybody alike. When people ask me about my future, all I have always had to tell them is that I will work hard till the end of time and keep improving the quality of my brand and its products. If I were to die tomorrow, I would only ensure that I have sweated enough today and that at least one thing about the organization has been changed for good. That is the beauty of it. Every business, or rather, everything we do in our entire lifetime, is some commitment that we show toward society. I also commit to my brand, and the brand apparently has a commitment toward its customers. Life becomes completely monotonous if a person has no responsibility for anything they do in their entire life. My growth is not just about my personal growth but the augmentation of my organization into a world-class brand.

The world is full of innovators and influencers impacting the lives of many people. From technology to business, these innovators have made a difference in the way we live today. Among them, Steve Jobs, Warren Buffett, and Narayana Murthy are my role models. They have inspired me to pursue my dreams and strive to make a difference in the world. Steve Jobs, the late CEO of Apple, was known for his ambitious and revolutionary ideas. He had a vision of taking technology to the next level and changing the way the world works. He was a creative genius, and his innovative products, like the iPhone and the iPad, were a testament to his ambition. It is a matter of fact that iPhones are the most sold mobile brand in the entire world, and I would happily confess that there are so many Apple products at my house, too. Jobs was a great leader who inspired his team to create something new and exciting. He taught us that with dedication and hard work, anything is possible. Warren Buffett, the legendary investor, is another one of my role models. He has made a fortune through his intelligent investments, and his success is a testament to his knowledge and experience. He is a great teacher who has given us valuable lessons about investing, such as the importance of diversification and the power of compounding. Buffett's success has also shown us the importance of patience and discipline in order to succeed. I have followed his example forever.

If I were an arrogant and impatient individual, I would have given up on so many things before it even started.

Narayana Murthy, the founder of Infosys, is my third role model. He is an inspirational figure who has transformed the Indian IT industry and made it one of the most respected in the world. His vision of creating a vibrant and competitive IT industry in India has been a great success.

He has also been a great advocate for corporate social responsibility, and his efforts have helped to improve the lives of so many people. He placed more importance on employees' salary and their lifestyles. He is the one who started paying employees fairly for their time and efforts.

I put maximum effort into acknowledging and appreciating my teammates by paying them well and providing bonuses, just the way Narayan Murthy does so that they feel empowered and satisfied.

All these three people, despite being the wealthiest people on the planet, are incredibly humble and down to earth. I have not even spotted them being complacent about the success they have achieved so far, and so am I. Learning from great personalities will make you think broader and more profound. I have never been arrogant or complacent about Royaloak's success to date.

I have always admired the Bhagavad Gita in addition to them. Through centuries, many people have found inspiration in the Bhagavad Gita. It is a timeless treasure, a source of wisdom and guidance. It is the conversation between Lord Krishna and Arjuna, a warrior on the battlefield of Kurukshetra. This conversation is about dharma, the path of righteousness. When Arjuna is faced with a difficult decision, he turns to Lord Krishna for guidance. Lord Krishna's words contain profound wisdom, which Arjuna and many others have used to make life-altering decisions. Lord Krishna's words are a beacon of hope in times of distress, providing insight and clarity. The Gita is more than just a philosophical text. It is evidence of the potency of compassion and love. Throughout the Gita, Lord Krishna speaks of the power of love and how it can help us to live a life of purpose.

He speaks of the importance of taking responsibility for our actions and the consequences of those actions. Gita is an epic that imparts the importance of honesty, and I have spent all my life following those lessons. Although I am more of a spiritual person rather than religious, I consider Krishna and Arjuna to be characters who have a lot to teach the world. It has helped me to stay focused on my vision. Everything that happens in our life has to be taken as an experience. I have never run after money as I knew that chasing money would only take it farther from my sight. What I always focused on was my vision, for I knew that my vision would earn me everything that I ever wanted.

It took me ages to come up with an actual vision for the company. I ensured to keep my mind clear and devoid of every sort of negative thought, for Krishna has always asked his disciples to manifest positivity over every odd of life.

With all this positivity, I made up my mind to deliver the best quality products to Royaloak's customers and made sure we had all the products that were required for every household. When we launched online stores during COVID-19 times, we ensured that all the products that were sold in the physical stores were available online, too. One thing about online shopping is that we only get to see the looks of the products; the customer gets to know about the quality only once it is delivered to their homes. If the product quality does not meet their expectations, they might get furious and may come up with and spread comments about the brand; hence, it is essential not to compromise on the quality. Not everyone around us gets the chance to travel overseas to experience the luxury of international goods, and for this reason, Royaloak made international import products available for everyone.

The current status of Royaloak's international expansion is that Mathan, my little brother, who is all grown up now to take on bigger responsibilities, is traveling to several countries to meet people to make room for Royaloak in their country. His wife, Preethi, who is my wife's younger sister, is another big pillar of support for the entire family. She is the one who helps Mathan whenever he slips into a situation of confusion or tension. Ever since she came to our family, everything started to feel even better.

It was like I had my own little sister whom I could talk to or seek advice from at times. I could see that my brother had become much more confident after knowing how well Preethi supported him. We ourselves cannot believe the distance we have covered so far in our entire journey. Life is full of surprises if you are willing to work hard. As the great Helen Keller once said, "Life is either a daring adventure or nothing at all." She knew that success comes from embracing the unknown and taking risks. The famous writer and philosopher Ralph Waldo Emerson once said, "Do not go where the path may lead; go instead where there is no path and leave a trail." Taking risks and working hard can open up a world of possibilities and opportunities and even lead to the most unexpected surprises. Mathan and I have always been ambitious and motivated to follow our dreams and desires. We come from a family who has always encouraged us to take risks and expand our horizons.

When we decided to expand our brand internationally, we were both confident as we knew our combined strength, courage, and determination could take us to places. We started off by meeting local business owners, entrepreneurs, and established professionals in the countries we were trying to expand our brand into.

We gathered as much information as we could about the market, the trends, and the competition. Then, as a team, we discussed the risks and rewards of our decision. We shared our stories, our successes and our failures, and the lessons we learned along the way. We felt empowered, knowing that we had each other's backs. With that confidence, we decided to take a leap of faith and invest in our brand. We made sure to spread our brand's message through various channels and platforms and worked tirelessly to build relationships with our customers.

Currently, Mathan has covered GCC countries like Oman and other countries such as Germany, Australia, and some African countries, and the best part is that we have received orders from all these countries.

We were ecstatic when we began to receive orders from around the globe. It was like finally getting to inhale some fresh air that suddenly blew into our lives, lifting us off our feet and propelling us forward with a newfound sense of optimism and vigor. Our business was like a seedling that had been carefully nurtured, and now, having taken root and grown into a sturdy tree, it is finally bearing the fruits of success. As a part of realizing our international dreams, we are more than excited to be opening our first international store within six months in any one of the countries mentioned. It will be an amazing experience for all involved, like a first-time skydiver jumping out of a plane- our heartbeats can be heard outside already as we are super excited for this event to happen.

This journey has been like a winding road with obstacles, dips, and curves. In several instances, it felt as if we were trudging through a thick fog, uncertain of what was ahead. But we kept pushing forward, like an ant carrying a crumb of food. We stumbled and faltered but never gave up. The journey was difficult but rewarding. We are proud of ourselves for never giving up, even in the face of adversity. We have come out of the journey stronger, wiser, and more prepared for the future. We have grown like a sapling that eventually turns into a tree, adding sense to the name of our brand, "ROYALOAK."

After all, like Lailah Gifty Akita once said, "The excitement of dreams coming true is beyond the description of words."

Takeaway:

Success is not something that only Narayana Murthy or Jeff Bezos can achieve. They all had humble beginnings and we all have the same amount of time every day. How you chose to use your time is completely up to you.

Live a disciplined life. Never deviate from your track, not even once.

Preethi (Mathan's wife)

I feel that both Mathan and Vijai are very unique in their own way. At times, I wonder if they are both like beasts or monsters. I am using words like beast and monster because their dedication level is unbeatable. The confidence that they have is something that no one could even imitate. I am not exaggerating, but as a matter of fact, not everybody can reach the extent where Mathan and Vijai stand right now. Their journey from poverty to where they are now is something that I cannot even explain in one word or sentence. It is hard to make people understand what it takes to be like these brothers. There were times when they had food just once a week. They rarely got the chance to have a nice meal. They went through lots of humiliation and frustration but still accomplished their dreams in the end, and I feel whatever they are having now is well deserved. As children, they never got anything they deserved or wanted, but today, I cannot help but say they are just genuinely amazing people.

My husband and his brother are very dedicated people, and they keep motivating themselves whenever they feel low. Even at times when I become a bit discouraged in doing something, Mathan becomes my true mentor; he says, "Preethi, I believe in your capability—can you assure me that you're willing to take this on? Because only you can do this!" and that is what keeps me motivated to perform well in my personal as well as professional life. They are just superb. If you ask me about the reason or secret behind their success, there is only one word – their hard work. They do a lot of homework. My husband's elder brother is his role model. Mathan follows everything that Vijai does, and the best part of their bond is that they inspire each other to do better. They keep improvising their skills and keep upgrading themselves to fit into the evolving world, and they never give up at any cost. They always think positively, no matter how challenging the circumstances are, and I believe that is one thing that made them accomplish a lot of things in their life. They are incredibly fearless and never think of the consequences that may arise from doing certain challenging things; they live in the present and make bold decisions.

Mathan used to tell me a lot about their childhood and all the struggles they had been through, and I used to think how great they were. I wonder how down-to-earth they are after achieving all this fame and wealth. I cannot even describe the depth of the pain they had to go through to reach where they are right now; hats off to their efforts! I first met Vijai and Mathan around nineteen years ago when Vijai came to our place to put forward a proposal for my sister Maheshwari for marriage. Our families liked each other, and soon, Maheshwari and Vijai tied the knot. I was pursuing my graduation back then, and within the next couple of years, our families thought that Mathan and I would make a great couple, which eventually led to our marriage. Although we never had any feelings for each other when my sister's wedding was happening, our families knew that we would make a great pair. But yes, I did feel that Mathan was a nice guy and that he was a hardworking individual, just like his brother. He liked me and wanted to invite me into his life, and for that, he waited for three long years until I graduated.

My sister and I never had any plans to get married to the same family; it was all a coincidence, and now, it is beautiful to realize that it was the best thing that has happened to us. Now that we all live inside the same house, I would say I feel really blessed. Maheswari is more like a mother to me. I can't always go to my hometown to visit my mother, but Maheshwari is giving me all the love and care, just like how our mother would do it.

I feel like I am always safe and protected when she is around. She is a very mature and sensible lady who can understand my feelings without even me having to say them out loud. It is fantastic to have a sister who can understand all my tantrums and still not get tired of me.

Vijai was more like a fatherly figure to me. Maheshwari and I did not have any brothers, and for me, Vijai was like my own brother more than a brother-in-law. I have immense respect for Vijai, and at times, I even get a bit nervous to talk to him, just like how daughters feel when they have to talk about some serious things with their fathers. We share an amazing bond and touchwood; nothing has affected it till this second. We support each other every single day. A couple of years back, when the business was going through a difficult phase, I told Vijai not to worry. We have always been each other's backbone, and that is one success secret of our family. We never use the word "no"; everything is possible if we stand together against the storm.

Although Mathan is younger than Vijai, I don't see much difference between them. Rather than differences, I would say there are plenty of similarities between them. They are equally strong and courageous. They never get scared of anything, and they enjoy experimenting with new things. It is the best feeling to see them grow every day. Royaloak is doing well only because of these two brothers and their commitment. I don't have a major role, nor have I contributed anything significant to Royaloak directly, but I have been supporting my husband and brother throughout their journey. We have been together in all the tough times because, sometimes, all that a person needs is someone to hold their hands when they are feeling low.

Royaloak is a growing company, and I believe not everyone can work with Royaloak. Only people who are passionate and have a fire burning inside them can be part of the team. It is not for those who are looking for a time pass or a temporary job. We only hire honest and dedicated people because that is how Mathan and Vijai are, and that is precisely why Royaloak has become South India's best furniture brand so far. I have always been so proud of these brothers; their strength and confidence are something that never fade away.

One of the most recent incidents that made me feel even more proud of them is the comeback they made after the COVID-19 outbreak. In the wake of the pandemic, I used to see Mathan and Vijai hosting meetings from nine in the morning to seven or eight in the evening. They hardly spent any time with us, and I was wondering what they were doing. But in the end, they proved that it is possible to succeed if you are ready to work hard.

Vijai and Mathan are not only great entrepreneurs but also really friendly fathers. They never stop the kids from doing anything. They ask us to never say no to the kids. Mathan says that it is ok even if they fall or get hurt. He says it is all part of their age and that we must never stop them from enjoying things, and I think that is how every father should be. Mothers are generally a bit worried about their kids' safety and would mostly be caring a lot and would probably encourage the kids to stay indoors, and even I am more like that. But Mathan and Vijai teach them life lessons and mold them perfectly as confident children. It feels incredible to see our kids growing up by adopting their father's qualities like confidence and positive thinking.

10

UNWRAPPING INSPIRATION: A CHAPTER FOR YOUNG MINDS

"The only way to do great work is to love what you do."
- Steve Jobs

India, a land renowned for its spirituality and boundless positivity, embraces a unique intertwining of cultures where every individual, regardless of their religion, is treated with equal respect and dignity. This vibrant nation is celebrated for its powerful manifestation techniques that have captivated the world's attention. Throughout history, India has consistently been at the forefront of development, and its enterprising spirit shines brightly through the brilliance of its people.

Indian entrepreneurs like Azeem Premji, the founder of Wipro, and Narayana Murthy, the co-founder of Infosys, have demonstrated exceptional leadership and vision. They have not only built successful enterprises but have also paved the way for others to follow. Their dedication, innovative thinking, and commitment to excellence have propelled them to great heights, earning them global recognition and respect. As you already know, being an aspiring individual, I find immense inspiration in the journeys of these two legends. I am confident that one day, my name will join the ranks of these iconic individuals, and the world will remember me as a great Indian entrepreneur.

There are millions of other Indians who are capable of becoming successful entrepreneurs. However, despite this wealth of talent, many individuals find themselves hesitant to take that crucial first step toward their dreams. Every year, India witnesses the birth of thousands of startups, attracting investments worth millions of rupees. Yet, tragically, the lack of courage often causes aspiring entrepreneurs to falter and fade away. As someone who has encountered numerous young individuals seeking professional guidance, I empathize with their apprehensions. I recall sharing with them the truth that I had no mentor to light my path, and my own success was driven solely by the power of positive thinking and unwavering courage.

Let me draw a parallel to the art of swimming. Imagine someone who fears the water, avoiding pools, beaches, and lakes due to their inability to swim. Will they ever conquer their fear of water without summoning the courage to take that leap? Trust me when I say that by mustering the bravery to jump into the pool, submerge themselves underwater, and hold their breath, a transformation begins to unfold. Within a few hours, a sense of liberation washes over them, dispelling their fears. The key lies in taking that pivotal first step and giving it a try.

Life itself is an intricate dance between trial and error. We encounter countless situations where failure looms ominously before us, ready to consume our hopes and aspirations. Yet, it is in those moments that we must summon the strength to resist and overcome.

Consider any life scenario. During our formative years, we may lack the culinary skills required to cook. Fear of fire and the specter of burns may haunt our thoughts. However, as we transition into adulthood, leaving the comfort of our homes to reside in hostels or other places, we find ourselves with no choice but to learn to cook. Gradually, we conquer our fears one step at a time, with courage serving as the essential ingredient in life's recipe.

Reflecting on my own journey, I vividly recall the day I purchased my very first four-wheeler, a Maruti OMNI 2222. Clueless about driving, I possessed only a rudimentary understanding of the steering wheel, a few pedals beneath the driver's seat, and the gear mechanism. Undeterred by my lack of knowledge, I approached the driver's seat, took a deep breath, and summoned all the courage within me.

Turning the key, I changed gears and pressed the accelerator. To my astonishment, the van began to move forward. My heart pounded like a drum, and the rush of wind against my face filled me with an exhilarating surge of energy. It was a defining moment, a testament to the power of taking that leap of faith.

Certain achievements may appear daunting, but remember, no one ever said they were impossible. If you aspire to lay the foundation stones of your entrepreneurial empire, I encourage you to forge ahead and embark on your journey.

In truth, only a mere 2% of people are deemed successful entrepreneurs, meaning that a staggering 98% do not achieve the desired outcome. When my first exhibition business encountered failure, I faced the risk of becoming just another statistic among the 98% of unsuccessful entrepreneurs. However, I refused to succumb to discouragement and pressed on.

Many individuals strive to earn enough to provide for their families, and when business ventures falter, they seek solace in conventional corporate jobs. It is understandable, as societal pressures, including those from their own families, often influence these decisions.

Parents may prioritize the stability of BPO jobs over their children's dreams, driven by the belief that money is a fundamental necessity for survival—and indeed, it is. However, it is essential to educate and enlighten them about the significance of nurturing dreams and aspirations. It is disheartening to note that 16% of the

Indian population still grapples with malnutrition and starvation, often paralyzed by fear of the unknown and their perceived limitations.

While my initial goal was to support my own family, I soon realized that my life held a grander purpose. As Royaloak evolved into a well-structured organization, it became a thriving family where thousands of individuals found a sense of belonging. The setback we faced in 2016 served as a wake-up call, reminding me that numerous families depended on our success. Filled with determination, I resolved to work tirelessly to protect their livelihoods for as long as possible.

In most companies, employees come and go, staying for a couple of years before moving on. Yet, our story is different. Within Royaloak, we have witnessed a remarkable phenomenon akin to government organizations. People have dedicated themselves to our mission for over sixteen years, fostering a sense of loyalty and camaraderie that is truly extraordinary.

As our company continues to grow, I recognized the opportunity to extend support to our vendors and logistics teams, who play an integral role in transporting our furniture. By expanding our network of vendors, we not only enhance their lives but also elevate the quality of our customer service, ultimately driving sales.

It is essential to shift our focus from a singular pursuit of monetary gain to a genuine desire to uplift others. By doing so, we experience profound personal satisfaction that transcends material wealth.

Success isn't merely a destination; it's a journey of envisioning, persevering through challenges, and nurturing a mindset steeped in positivity. I've always believed that one becomes what one consistently thinks. It's about those daily affirmations, those small yet significant steps taken each day that pave the way toward monumental achievements. I share this ethos with everyone I meet—encouraging them to start their day early at 4 am, dedicating 30 minutes to meditation, and harnessing the cosmic energy that greets us at dawn.

Why the early rise, you ask? There's a cosmic energy at play during those serene hours, an aura that lends itself to affirmations and visualizations, planting the seeds of success within us. Meditation, especially for half an hour, isn't just a practice; it's a gateway to tranquility and focus. It trains our minds to navigate the labyrinth of thoughts and channel them toward intuition, a potent force in achieving life's aspirations.

When it comes to business, I often ask a simple yet profound question: What truly defines success in the business world? The reality is stark—like I have already said before, only a mere two percent achieve what many aspire to. It's not for lack of careful planning, meticulous staff selection, or even a thoughtful product line. The missing piece often lies in focus and determination.

Most businesses, driven by the singular motive of profit, often fall short of their aspirations. The real secret lies not in chasing money but in fostering a vision rooted in clarity and passion. It's about impacting society positively, nurturing employees, and channeling unwavering dedication and focus into our endeavors.

Success isn't merely a byproduct of monetary gains; I believe money is the byproduct in reality. When these elements converge, when a business is propelled forward by a passionate vision that extends beyond profit margins, that's when true success blossoms. It's not just about what you do but the purpose behind it—the unwavering dedication to a cause larger than oneself. That, in essence, is the blueprint to real success in business and life.

When young minds approach me seeking guidance on what business path to embark upon, I often recall the wisdom of Thiruvalluvar, an ancient sage from Tamil Nadu. His words resonate through the ages, advocating a simple yet profound principle: do what you love. It's about offering to the world what you yourself seek—be it in quality, quantity, or price. This philosophy has been my guiding light throughout.

I advocate this approach to the younger generation, urging them to align their pursuits with their passions. But despite great vision and unyielding focus, many find success elusive. The truth is, not everyone is truly successful; many merely exist, drifting through life. The pathway to success isn't a proclamation of integrity alone; it's a practice that demands waking early, cultivating a positive mindset, and taming the racing thoughts that flood our minds each day.

Our minds are akin to spirited horses, racing with countless thoughts every day. Do you know how many thoughts cross through an average human brain every single day? We think about approximately sixty-thousand different things in a single day, believe it or not. You must mediate and bring your focus to the most important goals out of sixty-thousand every day in order to be able to succeed.

To find positivity, one must quiet this mental flurry. The key lies in the morning calmness, in that serene moment of communion with the divine. It's about expressing gratitude and embracing each challenge as a stepping stone to growth. I've faced numerous business hurdles, and each one has been a catalyst for my evolution. The morning ritual of gratitude shifts my perspective, fostering a contented spirit that attracts positivity.

Acknowledging the smallest blessings, from a cup of coffee to the love of family, sets the stage for positivity. It's about fostering an aura that draws in positive energies and people, leading to uplifting transactions and ventures. And amidst this journey, money isn't the linchpin; it's the vision of how much we contribute to others that propels our growth.

Success isn't just about personal gain; it's about the impact we have on the lives of others. Aligning our aspirations with service to others paves the way for a flourishing business. This, indeed, is the secret—cultivating a mindset of gratitude, channeling positivity, and dedicating our endeavors to serving others.

India's rich combination of spirituality, equality, and positivity has fostered an environment ripe for innovation and entrepreneurship. While the path may be daunting, it is crucial to summon the courage to take that initial step towards our dreams. Embracing defeat as a stepping stone to success and nurturing a spirit of resilience, we can navigate life's challenges and overcome our deepest fears. Let us remember that impossible is not a word synonymous with our aspirations. With unwavering determination, we can build not only successful businesses but also a better future for ourselves and those around us.

If you could build a routine and stick to it, I believe you can move way forward in life. Imagine a world where the first rays of dawn gently wash over the earth, and while most are still nestled in slumber, you rise with purpose. Wouldn't that be amazing? Every day, at the stroke of 3:30 am, before the sun graces the horizon, I wake up, attracting the cosmic energy, welcoming each new day with a sense of gratitude that resonates deep within my existence.

Before I reach for that glass of water, I pause, acknowledging the divine presence that guides my every step and the power that flows through my veins, illuminating my path and shaping my destiny.

Gratitude, a simple yet profound practice, has become the compass that steers my life's journey. It has propelled me forward, transforming obstacles into opportunities and setbacks into stepping stones. With each sip of water, I silently express appreciation for the abundance that surrounds me, setting the tone for a day filled with purpose and positivity.

After refreshing, I move to a cherished corner of my home where tranquility reigns supreme.

There, amidst the soft hues of morning light, I settle into stillness. With closed eyes and a calm mind, I slip into meditation that transcends the boundaries of time. As my breath becomes a rhythmic melody, a surge of energy courses through my veins, dissolving the inner conflicts that may have otherwise clouded my thoughts.

Just as a traffic light orchestrates the flow of vehicles, you have to envision the green light of positivity permeating your mind. With intention and focus, you attract the vibrant energy that banishes negativity, allowing your spirit to soar freely. The road ahead becomes clear, and with each breath, you inhale the essence of possibility and exhale the burdens that no longer serve you.

In harmony with the awakening of my mind, I turn my attention to the temple of my body. Yoga, a sacred practice that unites mind, body, and soul, is an integral part of my daily ritual. With graceful movements, I flow through asanas, stretching and strengthening my physical form.

Each pose becomes a symphony of balance and harmony, a dance of mindfulness that nurtures my body's well-being. As I synchronize my breath with motion, I feel a profound sense of alignment, as if every cell in my being vibrates with vitality.

The next vital factor that you need to pay attention to is your diet. Nourishment takes on a new meaning as you make conscious choices to fuel your body with wholesome sustenance. Instead of succumbing to the allure of processed and unhealthy foods, you have to embrace the healing power of nutrition. Each meal becomes an opportunity to infuse your body with vitality, choosing ingredients that nourish not only your physical form but also your mind and spirit. The food you consume becomes a symphony of flavors and nutrients, a source of sustenance that supports your holistic well-being.

With a disciplined and focused mind, I begin my work for the day, driven by a purpose that extends far beyond personal success. My gaze remains fixed on the horizon of service, for I know that my growth is intricately woven into the fabric of society. Each task, each endeavor, is infused with the intention to give back, to make a meaningful difference. It is in this wave of purpose that I find fulfillment, knowing that my actions have the power to touch lives and create ripples of positive change.

A disciplined life, you understand, is not an overnight accomplishment. It is a habit tightly tied with the threads of commitment, woven diligently day after day. It is a symphony composed of small, intentional acts that shape your character and mold your destiny. Through unwavering practice, you have to cultivate the art of observation and intuition, honing your ability to read the energies that surround you. As you navigate the complexities of human connection and the ever-changing landscape of life, your instincts serve as a compass, guiding you toward authenticity and aligning you with the right people and situations. In this dance of discipline, gratitude, and service, I discovered the true essence of a purpose-driven life.

In the realm of achieving greatness, there exists a powerful trait that transforms ordinary individuals into unstoppable forces. It is the tightly stitched discipline that sets them apart, propelling them to chase opportunities while uplifting and supporting others along the way. Such is the tale of Royaloak, a remarkable venture that began with a single investor—my mother. However, her investment was not monetary; it was an investment of love and unending faith.

As I embarked on my journey to Coimbatore, my mother displayed an extraordinary act of love. She willingly offered her entire savings, a testament to her belief in my abilities. To this day, I firmly believe that it is her love and prayers that continue to guide and bless my life, leading me down a path of happiness and fulfillment. Though she did not invest funds, her manifestation has had a profound impact on the business. Her support and motivation fueled my determination to persevere through challenges, and now I find myself inspiring and guiding other aspiring entrepreneurs.

In the pursuit of our dreams, it is vital to release worries about the outcome. The world is inherently designed to reward those who are willing to take risks. Just as watering a plant ensures its growth, consistent effort is the lifeblood of a successful business. Even though Royaloak has become a thriving brand, I remain committed to its daily operations. Each day, I make it a point to visit the office and connect with my teammates, inquiring about their well-being and experiences. I am driven by the belief that the idea of sitting back and relaxing while others work is unacceptable. No matter how large the organization grows, I strive to preserve the essence of its humble beginnings. The nurturing and care I provide to Royaloak mirror the love and dedication a parent has for their child. To parents, their children are forever cherished as tiny, vulnerable beings, regardless of their age or accomplishments. Likewise, all your customers and employees become part of your beautiful family.

I want people to remember me as a great leader and want them to learn a lot from me. When I made my grand entrance into this world, I provided the comedy with a good cry, and everyone had a good laugh. But when it's my grand exit, I hope to turn the tables and leave them all in tears – the kind you get from a heartfelt goodbye at the end of a great movie!

Takeaway:

Like I have already said, maintain discipline throughout your life. make it a habit and soon you will start feeling better. Feed your brain with positivity. Once your mind is in a happy space, everything will start falling in place.

CONCLUSION

No money? No problem! As long as you have a vision and the spirit to move forward, money doesn't really matter.

If you have a dream, you need to work towards it until you succeed; you have to protect that dream at all costs.

True richness is not solely determined by the circumstances of one's birth but rather by the unswerving commitment and focus one puts into shaping one's own destiny. Living a comfortable life is not a privilege reserved for the few but a culmination of tireless effort and unbeatable dedication.

Merely lamenting and casting blame upon our circumstances will yield nothing but emptiness. Instead, when we choose to rise above to embrace our challenges with unwavering determination, we discover the true essence of a fulfilling existence. Our lives come to a complete circle when we actively pursue our dreams, for it is through our deliberate actions that we truly earn the life we desire.

Had I been depressed or upset with everything life put me through, you would not even have known about me. I knew Singapore would be one hell of an ultra-luxury international experience, and I thought my life would change forever after that. I envisioned a day where my mother would wear an untorn saree, my father would drive a nice car, and my brother would go to the best university in the country. I hadn't planned anything for myself. All I wanted was for my family to be happy and safe. But life, in its unpredictable fashion, took an unexpected turn, shattering those dreams into countless fragments. In that moment of disarray, shock coursed through my veins, threatening to suffocate my spirit. Yet, I refused to succumb to the pain that threatened to consume me. I wasn't ready to live with the pain for the rest of my life. Like a phoenix emerging from the ashes, I found the strength to rise above the turmoil, to spread my wings wide and soar higher than anyone could have imagined.

After failing the first-ever exhibition, I could have wrapped it all up and stopped doing it forever. Well, that is what people usually do when their mind gets plagued with negativity and skepticism due to the intervention of other people. However, you must ignore them if you wish to grow in your career.

I want you to understand that no matter how difficult a thing looks, if it is meant to be, it will be. The more you manifest good things, the better your life becomes, and gradually, you will realize how great it is to watch things happening at the right time in the right flow as a result of your positive manifestation. As you know, when I first met Maheshwari, I had an inner feeling that she was made for me, or rather, let me say we were made for each other. She was the first person who caught my eyes like a magnet. I did everything in a year to ensure that her father accepted me, and here we are today, weaving our dreams together by simultaneously building our brand.

My journey has been one of both hardship and triumph, a symphony written in the language of resilience and unwavering determination. I recall the sting of failure and the bitter taste of disappointment as I stumbled in the early stages of my entrepreneurial endeavor. It would have been all too easy to surrender, to dig a hole and bury those dreams in the shroud of defeat. But I never did that. You must embrace failure as a stepping stone toward growth, as the catalyst that propels you toward greater heights. The world is replete with colorful hues and breathtaking vistas awaiting your exploration, and therefore, you should not get stuck in a place just due to the fact that you had to encounter a failure. You are deserving of the splendor that life has to offer, and it is within your power to seize it.

As I reflect upon my journey, I am reminded of the joy that accompanies the pursuit of one's passions. The path to success mostly would not be linear, and it is often marred by twists and turns that test the depths of our resolve. But it is in these moments of trial that we discover the true extent of our capabilities. You, dear reader, possess within you the capacity to surmount any obstacle, to defy the odds stacked against you. Never relinquish your guard, for the world can be a tempestuous sea, but within you lies the strength to defeat its storms.

And so, I conclude this chronicle of my rollercoaster ride —a journey that began in the depths of poverty but blossomed into a life of abundance and fulfillment. My story is not one of unattainable wealth but rather a testament to the power of hard work, perseverance, and unwavering belief in oneself.

Dear reader, as you close this book, may you carry with you the essence of my story—the knowledge that you, too, possess the power to transcend your circumstances to create a life that is both meaningful and fulfilling. Embrace the challenges that lie before you, for they are the stepping stones that lead to greatness. Let your dreams guide your path, and may the fire within your soul burn brightly, igniting your journey toward success.

Remember, dear reader, that your life is a canvas waiting to be painted with vibrant hues of possibility. Embrace your journey, embrace your dreams, and let the world bear witness to the magnificence that lies within you!

ABOUT THE AUTHOR

Vijai Subramaniam, the Founder & Chairman of Royaloak Furniture, is a renowned entrepreneur in the Indian business realm. Born in a dusty hamlet of Tamil Nadu state – 'Thevaram,' Vijai Subramaniam used to work while he was studying to support his family and row their boat off from the mouth of hardships to the brighter side. He had a kindling spirit to grow in life despite all the odds. He completed his graduation from a government college in the early 90s by simultaneously managing a tea powder business, which was his only source of income. He went on to host a number of exhibition businesses across South India, the first few being failures. But he was never discouraged by the initial blow. He continued to move forward, hoping for the best things to happen.

Being an optimist, a positivist, and a spiritualist, Vijai took every wrong turn and failure as a life lesson rather than being disheartened. He has been a speaker at numerous major entrepreneurial events held in different parts of the world. He is well known for his positive approach towards the young and the old alike. He educates and inspires young budding entrepreneurs by giving them recipes for success, which entrepreneurs are often secretive about. His goal is not just to sell furniture to the people in his country but to also provide an opportunity for them to experience the luxury of premium furniture. With Vijai's undulating dedication to the business, Royaloak is India's leading furniture brand today and is poised to be a global leader in the next few years.

www.ingramcontent.com/pod-product-compliance
Lightning Source LLC
LaVergne TN
LVHW011417080426
835512LV00005B/108